WITHDRAWN .

A12901 478995

Top Ten Myths in Education

Fantasies Americans Love to Believe

Larry E. Frase and William Streshly

I.C.C. LIBRARY

The Scarecrow Press, Inc.

Technomic Books
Lanham, Maryland, and London
2000

LA
217
.2
.F69
2000

SCARECROW PRESS, INC.
Technomic Books

Published in the United States of America
by Scarecrow Press, Inc.
4720 Boston Way, Lanham, Maryland 20706
http://www.scarecrowpress.com

4 Pleydell Gardens, Folkestone
Kent CT20 2DN, England

Copyright © 2000 by Larry E. Frase and William Streshly

All rights reserved. No part of this publication may be reproduced,
stored in a retrieval system, or transmitted in any form or by any
means, electronic, mechanical, photocopying, recording, or otherwise,
without the prior permission of the publisher.

British Library Cataloguing in Publication Information Available

Library of Congress Cataloging-in-Publication Data

Frase, Larry E.
    Top ten myths in education : fantasies Americans love to believe / Larry E.
    Frase and William Streshly.
        p.   cm.
    Includes bibliographical references (p.) and index.
    ISBN 0-8108-3770-6 (pbk. : alk. paper)
    1. Public schools—United States.   2. School improvement programs—
    United States.   I. Streshly, William A.   II. Title.
    LA217.2 .F69   2000
    370'.973—dc21   99–089743

∞ ™ The paper used in this publication meets the minimum requirements
of American National Standard for Information Sciences—Permanence of
Paper for Printed Library Materials, ANSI/NISO Z39.48-1992. Manufactured
in the United States of America.

CONTENTS

Foreword   v

Preface   vii

Myth 1: Schools Can Save Society   1
Myth 2: A National Standardized Testing Program Will
          Boost Achievement in America's Schools   15
Myth 3: Teacher Unions Have Helped Teachers and
          Education   27
Myth 4: School Boards Are Good for American
          Education   39
Myth 5: Self-Esteem Must Come First—Then Learning   57
Myth 6: Our Practices of Grouping and Grading
          Students Are Effective and Efficient   65
Myth 7: Public Schools Are Not Permitted to Teach
          Values   79
Myth 8: Teacher Evaluation Ensures High-Quality
          Instruction   93
Myth 9: Merit Pay for Teachers Is Unethical and Cannot
          Work   103
Myth 10: Large Schools Provide Quality Education
          Efficiently for Large Numbers of Students   117

Index   129

About the Authors   133

Notes and references by chapter

iii

FOREWORD:
THE CODE BUSTERS: EDUCATIONAL ANAGRAMS DECONSTRUCTED

The function of a myth is like an anagram in code. Although anagrams provide a message, they are really a transposition of other words and meanings. Professors Frase and Streshly are anagram breakers. They expose the top ten myths in education by decoding the anagrams and produce the counterfactuals that debunk the superficial messages by revealing the transpositions. Clearly, they are passionate about their code breaking.

I suspect that Frase and Streshly's passion is partly because they may have believed in some of the sacred cows they have now turned into hamburger in their almost four decades as practicing school administrators. Among the most potent are

- Schools can save society
- National testing can improve student achievement
- Learning is dependent on self-esteem
- Public schools cannot teach values
- Current methods of teacher evaluation can lead to improved-quality instruction
- The so-called economy of scale works in larger schools

Perhaps among the most persistent of the myths is that school quality can somehow be improved by "testing it in." I am reminded of an Iowa hog farmer who once told me, "You can't get a better hog by weighing it more often." This wisdom has somehow eluded the state legislators, who are convinced that more testing will dramatically improve education. Instead, we are documenting the decline of achievement in public education more precisely because we still pay homage to the myths Frase and Streshly debunk.

I like the format of the authors as they describe the content of the myths, why educators and the public continue to propagate them, the counterfactuals produced in their analysis, and the proposed solutions based on the deconstructed anagram.

Perhaps the most powerful function of the myths that Frase and Streshly debunk is to preserve the status quo. They essentially aim to consolidate the existing power base in education. The testing myth enhances the testing industry; teachers' unions work to enhance their stature and power, as do boards of education. These myths reinforce the perspective of those whose political power is represented in their framing of the issues that give rise to myths in the first place.

In this sense, the book is radical. The Latin derivation of radical is *root*, and Frase and Streshly return to the root of the myths. Although a person may not always agree with them, he or she will find their analyses thought provoking and refreshing. I invite you to turn the pages and remain a disinterested bystander. Like me, you will eventually take one side or the other. Who knows, perhaps you can think of alternative counterfactuals they missed. Such discoveries will keep this long overdue conversation going and hopefully lead to some radical changes instead of continuing the old nostrums being peddled by the same old sales force. We cannot see solutions to the old problems until we see the problems differently. The first step is to abolish the myths enshrouding them. We owe Frase and Streshly a debt of gratitude for their wisdom, perseverance, and common sense. So, dear reader, buckle down for a bumpy ride, because somewhere in this book there is something to offend nearly every vested interest in education today, yours included. You will not be disappointed.

Fenwick W. English
Professor and Program Coordinator, Educational Administration
Department of Educational Leadership and Policy Studies
College of Education, Iowa State University

PREFACE

The creation of American education was based largely on myth, and myths rule education today. The myth that gave birth to American education lies in the promise that education could cure America of its social diseases, street people, unemployment, and crime. Katz's research (1988, p. 113) offers potentially great insight into the beginnings of American education, the myths, and the mythmakers' motives. Education was oversold by a coalition of social leaders, status-anxious parents, and status-hungry educators to impose educational innovation, each for their own reason, upon a reluctant community (Katz, 1968, p. 218; also see Katz, 1975). In Massachusetts, school promoters were intimately connected with the economic transformation of the state. On the state level, James Carter, the first great advocate of school reform (Katz, 1968), based an argument for extended education on the fact that Massachusetts had to industrialize in order to survive (Report on the Education of Children in manufacturing establishments, 1846, Mass. House Document 49). Horace Mann railroaded a bill through the Massachusetts Legislature supporting and assisting railroad construction (Katz, 1968). It is no coincidence that both Carter and Mann vied for the position of state superintendent of schools (Messerli, 1865). Henry K. Oliver, the most vocal school promoter and a leading candidate for appointment as the third secretary of the Board of Education, was an agent for one of the largest cotton mills in the state. This was the former occupation of Joseph White, fourth secretary of the Board of Education (Jones, 1886). William Thorndike was one of the most active educational reformers in Beverly, Massachusetts. He was also a rich merchant (Stone, 1843). These men expended immense amounts of time and effort in their commitment to improve and extend public education. However, it is strongly documented that their motives were certainly not altogether altruistic. They had much to gain in finance and prestige (Katz, 1968). Education is not the only institution perpetrated by myth.

vii

Two other examples, prisons and insane asylums, were exposed by Foucault (1965, 1977, and 1980).[1]

In Pennsylvania, the push for compulsory education was fueled by promises that education likely could not and did not achieve. The report of the Board of Public Charities of the State of Pennsylvania (1871) included the following: "to diminish poverty and wretchedness, as well as ignorance, vice, and crime"; "the mere ability to read and write, by even an unskilled laborer, adds, on an average, from 25 to 50 percent to his value and efficiency"; the "number of prisoners will drop 10 percent."

Horace Mann (M. Mann, 1868) made similar promises for education when he was trying to "sell" education to American businessmen. He proposed that the returns on education "seemed to prove incontestably that education is not only a moral renovator, and a multiplier of intellectual power, but that it is also the most prolific parent of *material riches*" (p. 109, emphasis added). The U.S. Government Bureau of Education, in a bulletin entitled "The Money Value of Education" (1917), posited this argument again in 1917.

Early and mid–nineteenth century promoters of compulsory education argued that the public education system would attack five major problems: urban crime and poverty; increased cultural heterogeneity; lack of training and discipline in an urban and industrial workforce; homeless, unemployed, and nonproductive youth; and the anxiety among the middle classes about their adolescent children (Katz, 1988, p. 102). These problems were portrayed by the upper-middle and upper classes as an epidemic of lawlessness and pauperism threatening the foundation of morality and the maintenance of social order. These problems, as Katz (1988, p. 118) explained, appear to be products of capitalist development. In essence, the promise was that school systems would transform the habits of the population to match the emerging and radically new social and economic order. The reality is that education, as designed, failed to fulfill these promises (Katz, 1988).

Myths and American Education: *Cui Bono?*

Myths do not occur by chance. Sometimes a bit of reality sparks an idea, only to be adopted and cultivated by a needy person or group of people in search of understanding.[2] Other times, a myth is created for profit and gain rather than to benefit those it is purported to serve. In education, the self-interested representatives of gentry classes attempted to impose their schemes on a reluctant populace and make the school into an agency that would at once promote their own economic well-being and render workers and immigrants socially safe. The motives for manufacturing myths are not so much the theme of this book as are exposing and dispelling widespread current practices as myths. The purveyors of the myths that built American education in the eighteenth and nineteenth centuries benefited personally at the expense of possibly more effective educational reform for children. Prestige, power, and money were their rewards.

Myths continue to rule public education. Just as the assumed orbit of the Sun around the Earth hindered progress of astronomy as a science, widely held myths stymie and preclude educational reform. The ruling aristocracy threatened Galileo with severe punishment if he did not recant his then sacrilegious claim that the Earth revolved around the Sun. After all, people were comfortable with the incorrect belief that the Sun orbited the Earth. It *worked* for the politicians. To state otherwise brought great discomfort and threatened the pious nobility. This historical snippet sounds medieval. Could such fact-bending skulduggery happen today? It could. It did. In fact, a cover-up similar to that which kept Galileo's finding in the dark occurred in 1991, when the federal aristocracy threatened some of the nation's finest scientists and statisticians with economic sanctions if they did not bury a finding.

The case involves the Sandia National Laboratories, the workplace of some of America's finest scientists and statisticians. These were the days following the Ronald Reagan administration's highly touted report on the nation's schools (*A Nation at Risk*, 1980). Conventional wisdom held by Reagan and then by President George Bush was that public education was an utter failure—U.S. student achievement was behind most other countries and was getting worse. Secretary of State James Watkins said he wanted scientists to be involved in fixing science education, and an academic named Mike Wartell, currently chancellor of Indiana-Purdue University at Fort Wayne, was put in charge.[3] Wartell challenged the Sandia system analysts to determine the performance level of the nation's educational system. Was it up? Was it down? Was it level? After months of high-powered analysis, the scientists told Wartell that the Bush administration's statements about student achievement were *wrong*. They said that American education was doing quite well. In fact, they said that *each racial group's score on the SAT had actually gone up during the period in question* (Carson, Huelskamp, and Woodall, 1991). The fact that scores were down was illusory. The reason? More students from low-achievement groups and women (math bias) were taking the test than before. The effect was that the overall score was lower, but the performance for each pentile was higher—a simple case of statistical regression. The increased numbers of students from low-achievement groups and women taking the test influenced the overall mean.[4]

The seriousness of the supposed decline in test scores was strengthened by the claim that the cost of education had increased greatly. The Sandia personnel found that this was true, but with one crucial caveat. The price of regular education had remained level, while the cost and number of students in special education had increased manyfold (see chapter 6, on grading and grouping). In other words, educational funding for more than 90 percent of the nation's students had been frozen, while services to the disabled skyrocketed. Naturally, any effect of this money would not be reflected in the Scholastic Aptitude Test (SAT) since special education students usually do not take the test. (For a technical analysis of the topic, see *The Manufactured Crisis*, by Berliner and Biddell, 1995.)

What happened to these findings by prize-winning American scientists? Were they printed in newspapers and magazines? In only a few isolated cases. Why did they remain hidden? The existing "aristocracy," like the aristocracy of Galileo's time, was not comfortable with the findings: the facts did not support the widely publicized myth and political agenda. Based on what followed, it certainly appears that they wanted to bury the findings of the scientific community in order to perpetuate the myth that education was an out-and-out failure and in need of major reform.

The team was asked to brief a group of assistant secretaries of education on the study. On hearing the briefing, the secretary of energy accusingly queried, "Who allowed them to do that?" Before the word spread, Senators Robert Dole and Pete Domenici asked them to brief the Republican leadership of the Senate, including Dole, Domenici, David Kearns (undersecretary of education), Lyn Chaney (head of the National Endowment for the Humanities), and Assistant Secretary of Education Diane Ravitch, among others. Following the briefing, David Kearns said, "Bury this report or I'll bury you." The next message directed to the Sandia National Laboratory was *"get out of education.* Your funding is threatened" (see note 1).

Yes, the Venetian aristocracy's style of threat to the bold and irreverent Galileo was repeated in 1991. Yes, right here in the United States of America! Test scores were not going down, and the myth was actually being promulgated and nourished by the government. The skulduggery of ancient times continues into the twentieth century. Exposing myths like these and how they are killing education is the purpose of this book.

Myths That Are Killing Public Education in the United States

The chapters in this book are not affiliated with any political agenda or reform campaign. The myths we expose in turn expose many long-lived yet debilitating sacred cows. Their existence has served powerful individuals and pressure groups for decades, but they have not served education. They not only stymie educational progress, they preclude it.

Many superintendents recognize these myths. Some lack the intestinal fortitude to speak out. Many who did, lost their jobs. Knowing that they must survive to make any difference at all, many superintendents choose less risky tactics. Frontal attacks on the myths most cherished by society and board members are professional suicide. Thus most astute administrators trim to a middle course. They recognize the evils spawned by the myths and use various strategies to minimize their deleterious effects.

We are resolute in our belief that public education can be the best form of education. We are equally resolute that major improvement is needed. This book was not written to knock education, as so many others have. We do not publish this book hoping to capitalize on negativity about education. There is far more than enough faultfinding, and much of it is unfair and unfounded. The press is the major source of brickbats about education. David Berliner recently referred to their "painful penchant to publish negative articles" as "if it bleeds, it leads." If it tears at the heart of public education, if it can draw blood, it will be a lead article.[5] The positive stories are seldom given coverage. We know that much of the negative news is distorted and improperly portrayed and is given coverage at the expense of reporting the good news.

The reality, of course, is that all is not well in education. Literacy continues to be a problem, and achievement test scores should be higher. Some staunch and well-spoken supporters of public schooling have apparently given up. Witness the late Albert Shanker's interview in the *New York Times*. In desperation and frustration with progress, he said, "Blow up the schools" (Woo, 1996). It appeared on the front page of the *New York Times Magazine*. We do not want to blow up the schools; far from it. But we do want to blow up the myths that prevent major increases in productivity.

It should be said at the outset that this book does not purport to tackle the legitimate problems faced by American public schools. The disintegration of the nuclear family, the impact of massive poverty, the despicable condition of many American inner-city schools, and the failure to ensure a textbook in each subject area for each student—these are the real challenges that American society must address. William Raspberry (1999) captured the essence of the problem perfectly when he asserted that closing achievement gaps can only be accomplished if parents (and parents to be) "boost their youngsters' intellectual development, socialization and self-confidence—beginning at birth." This book focuses instead on errors in our belief systems that confound, obfuscate, and ultimately prevent efforts by educators to address the legitimate educational problems.

Purposes and Definitions of Myth

The word "myth" is derived from the Greek word *muthos* and has a wide range of meanings. However, the most common is something chosen, a story, either fictional or based on knowledge and logic. Whatever the definition, myths communicate sacred events or other beliefs and have a linkage in history. Although myths are sometimes forced upon people, at other times people have the privilege of selecting a myth and rejecting others based on their individual temperament and inclinations (Genovese, 1996).

When examining the purpose and value of a myth, at least two questions must be answered: What is the content of the myth? and What is its function? Is the content accurate, false, or somewhere in between? Many myths, such as Santa Claus delivering presents to every household on Christmas Eve, are obviously fairy tales, a form of myth. The content is obviously incorrect, but many Christians and some members of other religions appreciate its function in that it keeps a mystery and the spirit of Christmas alive for our children, and for adults it keeps a satisfying tradition alive. Myths such as these are nurtured by the populace because they are pleasant and do not cause major ill effects. Consider the Greek myths. Plato firmly believed that his country's ancient myths were fabrications designed to communicate a lesson on morals or to teach an ethic (Hamilton and Cairns, 1961). But when asked if the government should tell the citizenry of the false content, he said no. Instead, he suggested that the myths serve a good function—they communicate nationally held beliefs and teach morals and ethics that hold the Greek society together. The function was considered good. Exposing the stories as fiction would lead to great insecurity and confusion.[6]

Complexity deepens when we consider the functions of myths. Some myths are apparently perpetuated for the greater good, for example, Plato's example above, while others are perpetuated for personal or ideological gain. Consider the mythology that has grown around the IQ test. Tests related to the IQ test are used to select applicants for admission to universities and sundry other cherished institutions and make definitive lifetime decisions about individuals' potential to learn. The reality is that Alfred Binet (1975) devised the original test to identify students who needed special instruction, whether gifted or feebleminded, to succeed in school (Cubberley, 1948). The tests were used to sort students by intelligence (Cremin, 1988). Binet never said that his test measured intelligence: "We must protest and react against this brutal pessimism" that "intelligence of an individual is a fixed quantity, a quantity that one cannot augment" (cited in Weissglass, 1998). He also said "it is an attempt to do for democratic forms of national organization what a two-class school system does for monarchical forms, but to *select intellectual capacity from the whole of mass of the people, rather than from a selected class or caste* (cited in Cubberley, 1948, p. 821; emphasis added).

Columbia University was among the first institutions to use intelligence tests as part of the admissions procedure, and their application in this way was influenced by myths regarding the mental skills of persons newly arrived in America. A grand example is Columbia University President Nicholas Murray Butler's proclamation that the 1917–1918 class was depressing in the extreme in that it was made up of foreign-born and children of those but recently arrived in this country. He was instrumental in establishing the College Board (Weissglass, 1998). This apparent attack on immigrants was strengthened by Brigham's (1923) conclusion that "the average intelligence of our immigrants is declining" (p. 197), a statement that rings loudly in today's newspaper stories. At minimum, such contentions are distasteful. At full value they are discriminatory, racist, cognitively wrong, and philosophically deranged—the value, to preserve privilege.

The Top Ten Myths addressed in this book are not benign and beneficial, as are fairy tales. The Top Ten Myths are causing great harm to education; eventually, if not stopped, they will kill public education. These myths have strong historical roots. For instance, Myth 4 deals with school boards. To argue against the efficacy of school boards may seem sacrilegious and a slander against Americans' fundamental belief in local control. However, the current form of local control—school boards—is throttling educational progress. School boards and the manner in which they conduct themselves are the issue, not local control. Similarly, testing can be a very valuable activity. Testing can provide data that educators and parents can use to assess student learning and plan further instruction. As we show in Myth 2, most state-mandated, test-score comparisons do not inform instructional practice. The comparisons are too often used by politicians to further their political future. A perfect example is California's 1998 Proposition 227 that required immigrants, who have not yet had an opportunity to learn to speak or read English, to take an achievement test in English. Worse, those who supported this were unwilling to compromise (for example, give the children one year to learn and then test in English). The possible answers to why anyone would support this practice are staggering and divisive.

Criteria for Selecting the Top Ten Myths

Selecting the Top Ten Myths was not easy, and ultimately the selection process was somewhat subjective. We conferred with the fates, gods, pedagogical experts, laypeople, and each other to divine the Top Ten Myths. But to no less degree we relied on our many years of experience as public school teachers, public school administrators, superintendents, consultants, curriculum management auditors, and researchers and authors in the professorate.

This book is not part of a grand political scheme for reform. It is ad hoc. The only purpose is to expose myths that retard educational improvement. Our years as superintendents of schools total twenty-four. Our years as assistant principal, principal, and in other administrative positions total fifteen. Our years in the public schools total fifty. Our years as professors total twenty-three. We relied on these experiences and the thousands of discussions in schools and the professional literature. We also relied on what we observed as curriculum management auditors in more than sixty large and small school districts. Conducting the audits gave up-close exposure to the classrooms, teachers, students, parents, politicians, administrators, policies and procedures, and the work of school personnel and boards of education.[7] These are our databases.

Many myths about education exist, and we used six stringent criteria as the acid tests to sort out the top ten. The six criteria are as follows:

1. The myth must send researchers and reformers on thousands of wild-goose chases and obscure a pathology.
2. It cannot be driven by circumstances beyond education's control.
3. It must cause huge sums of money to be wasted.
4. It must impede student learning.
5. It must obscure partisan special interests.
6. Finally, the myth must affect a large majority of schools and students.

Our riposte to the myths that do so much harm is to expose them for all to see. They are not divine, not in any way. They are harmful, and for harmful reasons many people work to prolong them and their negative effects.

Some prominent myths and widely held topics were not chosen because they did not meet our criteria. For instance, among the widely held ideas that were not chosen are busing and technology. The ideas that forced busing ends or even seriously reduces segregation and that it leads to increased achievement are myths. Forced busing is an utter failure, but it continues. However, it was not picked in the top ten because it affects a limited number of districts, does not significantly impact educational performance, and was mandated by court orders beyond education's control. Technology, with its accompanying fanfare, also was not chosen. It is widely popular, but the jury on effectiveness is still out. Although the belief that it is a panacea is certainly a myth, we firmly believe that technology has an important role in school improvement. However, it is extraordinarily unlikely that technology will live up to its many promises for student achievement.

In every case, rectifying the anomalies that stem from the Top Ten Myths will produce immediate and dramatic improvements. In *every case*, the reforms would *cost the taxpayer nothing*. In fact, our calculations reveal that dispelling all of the Top Ten Myths would catapult America's public school performance far ahead of its nearest competition—for less money than we are currently spending! Sound impossible? Read on.

Acknowledgment

Artwork in the book is by Christian Hansen at Chyll Productions. E-mail to drchyll@chyllproductions.com or visit my website www.chyllproductions.com.

Notes

1. Foucault (1965, 1977, and 1980) contends that their founders indeed believed in their efficacy but argues that their promises were obviously too bold, too strident. Based on scant evidence, they were touted as quick fixes to vexing social problems, yet the purveyors of the myth promised that they would cure the individuals they housed. If the myth caught on, the purveyors would wield power and authority over others, make their living, and enjoy prestige and fame (Foucault, 1980). Insane asylums and modern rehabilitation-orientated prisons did catch on and obviously serve a purpose; they rid, at least temporarily, the streets of dangerous and mentally sick people, but they failed to achieve their promise—curing them. This was very clever, because in substituting a service (for example, getting criminals off the street temporarily) for the grandiose promise of reforming criminals, prisons won a self-perpetuating place in society. In failing to fulfill their promises, they were assured of a huge market of return clientele—recidivists. Even though the perpetuators failed to do as promised, they found a place of lasting importance.

2. For a thorough discussion of the variety of definitions myths and the debates regarding religion and other sociological implications, see M. Day (1984), *The Many Meanings of Myth*, New York: University Press of America; S. Ausband (1983), *Myth and Meaning, Myth and Order*, Macon, GA: Mercer University Press; K. Jaspers and R. Bultmann (1969), *Myth and Christianity* (translated by N. Guterman), New York: Noonday Press; J. MacQuarrie (1969), *The Scope of Demythologizing*, Glowacester, MA: Peter Smith; E. N. Genovese (1996), *Mythology: Texts and Contexts*, Third Edition, New York: McGraw-Hill; D. Leeming (1998), *Mythology:*

The Voyage of the Hero, Third Edition, New York: Oxford University Press; B. Mali-
nowski (1984), *Magic Science and Religion and Other Essays*, Westport, CT: Green-
wood Press.

3. This explanation of events regarding the Sandia report was gained from a
series of interviews with Dr. Mike Wartell, chancellor, Indiana-Purdue University–Fort Wayne, Spring 1998.

4. For additional debate regarding the Bush administration's handling of the
Sandia report, see D. Berliner and B. Biddell (1995), *The Manufactured Crisis*, Reading, MA: Addison-Wesley.

5. Data supporting Berliner's statement is provided in his 1997 address to the
American Education Research Association Annual Conference, "If It Bleeds, It
Leads."

6. This is paraphrased from Plato's Law X 884–887 (see *Dialogues*, edited by E.
Hamilton and H. Cairns [1961], New York: Pantheon Books).

7. The Curriculum Management Audit was developed by Fenwick W. English.
Its primary rationale is based on the assumed alignment between the written curriculum, for example, curriculum guides and texts; the taught curriculum, for example, what the teachers teach; and the tested curriculum, for example, the con-
tents of the tests. For detailed reading regarding the Curriculum Management
Audit, see Frase, English, and Poston (1994).

References

A Nation at Risk: The Imperative for Educational Reform. (1983). Washington, DC: U.S.
    Department of Education, National Commission on Excellence in Education.
Berliner, D., and B. Biddell. (1995). *The Manufactured Crisis*. Reading, MA: Addi-
    son-Wesley.
Binet, A. (1975). *Idees Modernes Sur Les Enfants*. Trans. S. Heisler. Menlo Park, CA:
    Suzanne Heisler.
Brigham, C. (1923). *A Study of American Intelligence*. Princeton: Princeton Univer-
    sity Press.
Carson, C., R. Huelskamp, and T. Woodall. (1991). *Perspectives on Education in
    America: Annotated Briefing—Third Draft*. Albuquerque, NM: Sandia National
    Laboratories, Systems Analysis Department.
Cremin, L. (1988). *American Education: The Metropolitan Experience, 1876–1980.*
    New York: Harper and Row.
Cubberley. (1948). *The History of Education*. Cambridge, MA: Riverside Press.
Foucault, M. (1965). *Madness and Civilization: A History of Insanity in the Age of Rea-
    son*. New York: Random House.
Foucault, M. (1977). *Discipline and Punish: The Birth of the Prison*. Trans. A. Sheri-
    dan. New York: Vintage.

Foucault, M. (1980). In C. Gordon (ed. and trans.), *Power/Knowledge: Selected Interviews and Other Writings by Michel Foucault, 1972–1977*. New York: Pantheon.

Frase, L., F. English, and W. Poston. (1994). *The Curriculum Management Audit*. Lancaster, PA: Technomic Publishing.

Genovese, E. N. (1996). *Mythology: Texts and Contexts* (3rd ed.). New York: McGraw-Hill.

Gould, S. (1996). *The Mismeasure of Man*. New York: Norton.

Hamilton, E., and H. Cairns (eds.). (1961). *Dialogues: The Collective Dialogues of Plato, Including the Letters*. New York: Pantheon Books.

Jones, H. (1886). "Henry Kemble Oliver," in Commonwealth of Massachusetts, *Seventeenth Annual Report of the Bureau of the Statistics of Labour*, March, p. 3047.

Katz, M. (1968). *The Irony of Early School Reform*. Cambridge: Harvard University Press.

Katz, M. (1975). *Class, Bureaucracy, and School*. New York: Praeger Publishers.

Katz, M. (1988). "The Origins of Public Education: A Reassessment," in B. McClellan and W. Reese, *The Social History of American Education*. Chicago: University of Illinois Press.

Mann, H. (1886). *Life and Works of Horace Mann*. Vol. 3. Boston: Horace B. F. Fuller.

Messerli, J. (1865). "James G. Carter's Liabilities as a Common School Reformer." *History of Education Quarterly* 1:14–25 (March).

Raspberry, W. (1999). "Before Headstart." *Washington Post*, November 12, p. A35.

Report of the Board of Public Charities of the State of Pennsylvania (1871).

Report on the Education of Children in Manufacturing Establishments. (1846). Massachusetts House Document 49 (March 7).

Stone, E. (1843). *History of Beverly, Civic and Ecclesiastical, from Its Settlement in 1630 to 1842*. Boston: published privately.

U.S. Bureau of Education Bulletin. (1917). "The Money Value of Education." Bulletin 22.

Weissglass, J. (1998). "The SAT: Public-spirited or Preserving Privilege?" *Education Week* 17:31 (April 15), p. 60

Woo, E. (1996). "Blow Up the Schools: Albert Shanker's Last Stand." *New York Times Magazine* (December 1), p. 17.

Introduction

As we all know but likely take somewhat for granted at this point, the masses of people who immigrated to America wanted a new life. They wanted to create a new society that offered freedom and self-rule and all the related benefits for the people: life, liberty, and the pursuit of happiness. Newcomers from England sought to avoid civil strife; Puritans, Quakers, Mennonites, Anabaptists, and Huguenots sought freedom of worship; nearly all sought an economy where they could make a living for their families and avoid wars. They found promise for these hopes in America. But they fully knew that one of the keys was education—their children must be literate so that they could read the laws of their new land and their chosen book of worship. The purpose of education was clear and *focused*. It was to teach children how to *read* so that they could take their places as upstanding, moral members of society.[1]

The founding fathers did it in spades. They started an education system that delivered the richest and most powerful nation in the world, a nation where people experienced freedom of religion, the opportunity to pursue happiness and work for profit, and a homeland where people could gather to debate politics and to socialize. As is always the case, astounding growth in population brought with it an increase in problems and an explosion of new expectations for the schools. Increasingly, America turned to the schools as either the solution or the means for the solution of all problems.

The Myth

The myth—that the public schools can and should do it all—is illustrated by the ever-open arms of the not-so-realistic confidence of educators shown in the cartoon. We contend that they cannot solve the social ills of our nation. As the sweltering masses of immigrants continued to come to America in the late nineteenth century, reading remained crucial, but schools inherited the job of stabilizing a nation of diverse ethnicity and teaching the ways of the new country. In short, the schools were to Americanize the immigrants.

From its humble beginnings of teaching the three Rs, the expansion of the schools' responsibilities grew geometrically, in number and scope. Many were never envisioned by our forefathers—desegregating racial groups, teaching safe sex, dealing with teenage pregnancy, keeping kids off the streets, and preventing violence are a few in the long list. The following is offered as a brief list summarizing the voluminous and unrealistic new responsibilities assigned to and accepted by the schools during the past 150 years. The list illustrates our belief that schools have lost their focus, that society expects them to do things they are not capable of, and that the widely diverse expectations have rendered education incapable of doing anything well.

- In the 1600s, the Calvinists sought to teach reading so that young people could read the laws of the new land and their books of religion. Teaching reading was the purpose of schools; to engender ethical character was the outcome.

- In the 1870s, the purpose was expanded to include the classics such as Latin, Greek, English, Earth science, physical sciences, and higher mathematics.

- Beginning in the early 1900s and through 1930, John Dewey's progressive education dominated, and schools' responsibilities were greatly expanded. In an attempt to teach the *whole child*, the schools added vocational skills, physical fitness, citizenship, family duties, consumer skills, leisure activities, *values clarification activities*, rational abilities, fine arts, worthy home membership, and worthy use of time to the curriculum.

- The shift to Dewey's progressive education was reversed in the 1930s through the 1950s, and the academic curriculum was emphasized. However, all of the previous responsibilities were still in place. After World War I, the Cold War, and Sputnik, the emphasis on social goals lost favor. They were not eliminated, just put on the back burner. Historian Arthur Bestor said, "Concern over personal problems has grown so excessive as to push into the background what should be the school's central concern, the intellectual development of students." Wernher von Braun said, "End family life and human relations education. Adopt the European system, focus on technical and scientific subjects and academic excellence." Admiral Hyman Rickover said, "De-emphasize life adjustment schools and progressive educationalists." After his study of high schools, the eminent James Conant advised providing "good general education for all and emphasize educating those with a talent for handling advanced subjects." Further, he recommended tightening standards and grades, emphasizing mathematics, science, and languages, and grouping students according to ability. With these messages, couched in terms of a free people surviving in a world where communism was a threat, the federal government was pleased to give billions of dollars to fund training for teachers, design programs for the children gifted in the maths and sciences, and beef up these subjects for all students. These were in addition to providing a good general education for all. None of the previously assigned responsibilities were deleted. Thus, gifted students became the first group of American students targeted by law to receive special programming in schools.

- The schools' role in health care heightened in the late 1950s. (We remember receiving our polio vaccines and being tested for tuberculosis.)

- The 1960s saw racial injustice and major strides to correct it. In the presence of tremendous urban riots and national unrest, President Lyndon B. Johnson pledged to create the Great Society, where equality and equity would prevail, where no person would be disadvantaged. Schools were assigned the responsibility for solving much of the racial unrest. Courts ordered schools to desegregate, that is, to bus students to achieve racial balance. They were ordered to end segregation and attain equality and equity for all students, regardless of race. Equal opportunity legislation and affirmative action polices became the emphasis of the decade.

- Spurred by the perceived injustices and outright stupidity of the Vietnam War, the schools returned to progressive education emphasized by value clarification activities; mantras about making love, not war, and soul power; and encounter groups. Unfortunately this was a time when pop music priests would overdose and pop psychological nostrums about self-actualization would prove unattainable. To enhance students' understanding of urban and campus riots, university professors brought marijuana to classrooms for students to smoke. Elementary schools said that self-respect and self-direction were their primary goals for students. This decade in public schools and universities was thus popularly dubbed the "touchy–feely era." Mastering subject matter was not eliminated as a responsibility, but it was secondary in kindergarten through graduate school. Courses on active listening, exploring values, and feeling good about yourself popped up across North America. These topics became the theme of existing courses, too. (We experienced an advanced statistics course in the early 1970s, the theme of which was "exploring how we feel about statistics.") Learning how to use tests of significance and interpret the results was not nearly so important as airing feelings about societal injustices and how they may harm our psyches. Solving social unrest and metaphysical issues dominated the curriculum.

During this period of deep thinking, test scores fell, just as they did in the 1920s, and the public again began to lose confidence in the schools. Simultaneously, James Coleman and his colleagues (1965) completed his study of educational equality for Congress. The report fueled antieducationists' fire. Coleman essentially said that student achievement was primarily dependent on the family's socioeconomic status and the little known concept of locus of control, a personality variable describing whether people see their future being controlled by themselves or powers beyond their control (Bridge, 1979). Further, the conclusion was that the funding level of the schools, teachers' experience, quality and quantity of equipment, and all the rest make no difference. With all of this plus the dramatic decline in test scores during the late 1960s and early 1970s, public respect for schools hit an all-time low.

- Enter President Reagan, Secretary of Education William Bennett, and *A Nation at Risk*, a report seeking a longer school day, greater focus on homework, stricter grading standards, higher expectations for students, and a focus on basics. The shift back to basics was on. Bennett announced his ideal curriculum for the hypothetical James Madison High School: English, foreign languages (Latin, Greek, and so on), hard sciences, classical literature, and higher mathematics. Look familiar? Indeed, the classical curriculum of the 1870s through 1900 is nearly identical. Through the eighteenth and nineteenth centuries the pendulum has continuously swung between the classical curriculum and progressive education.

  The 1970s witnessed an explosion in the number of high school–age pregnancies, a liberalization of sexual mores, and greater frequencies of venereal diseases. By the mid-1980s nearly every school district in America had a sex education curriculum. Soon the need became greater. The threat of AIDS dominated sex education classes. Safe sex had to be taught by the schools. Schools distributed condoms. Sexual orientation, the gay community, and education regarding homophobia entered the curriculum. Certainly those who began education in America did not envision these as a responsibility of the schools.

- Other major social changes continued in American society and had profound impact on the schools' responsibilities. The battle cry against the Caucasian male-gender-dominated society expanded. Women's rights issues entered the curriculum. Gender discrimination was to end, and it was the schools' responsibility to make it happen. Education on gender bias entered the curriculum.

- In 1974, the U.S. Supreme Court stated in *Lau v. Nichols* that schools "must help those who are certain to find their classroom experience wholly incomprehensible because they do not understand English." The focus on non-English speakers in schools was further emphasized by the 1986 Bilingual Act. Schools were ordered to teach children in their native language, at least for a few years. For large school districts like New York and Los Angeles, where the student body may represent seventy different languages including Hmong, Laotian, and Vietnamese, this was a major challenge. But the demand was clear: schools must find a way to deliver instruction in students' native languages.

- In 1975 another group of disadvantaged people was added to the schools' list of responsibilities. Congress passed Public Law 94–142 requiring the schools to provide special services for children with physical and mental disabilities of all kinds and degrees. This act has resulted in greatly enlarged responsibilities for schools, with woefully inadequate funding. Fully certified administrators and teachers in each specialization were needed. As noted in the Preface, special education absorbed huge quantities of energy and money, with little to show for the effort.

These plus many responsibilities were heaped upon the schools. Others include door-to-door or block-to-block bus service; preschool care; medical checkups; disease immunization; eye, hearing, posture, and dental check services; free breakfasts; free lunches; school nurses; condom distribution and sexual counseling; parent education; home checks; after-school care; and services to private schools. We even experienced a mandate to inspect hair follicles for lice. Yes, we found lice. Yes, we treated the subject children. And yes, they returned to school the next week with, yes, lice. All at the expense of the academic program. The point is that another agency should have been in charge of lice eradication, while we ensured learning.

Consider just how easy and whimsical it is for new subjects to be added to the curriculum. During World War I, military officers noted that some American soldiers ran in the face of enemy fire. After the war Congress decided that this was not good and said we need to teach appreciation of American history. Thus, the venerable American history course is in the curriculum, often displacing world history. During World War II, officers noted that American boys were not as physically fit as they should be. Congress ordered physical education for all American youth in order to be ready for the next war. In the 1970s teen pregnancy rates went up. State legislatures mandated sex education.

The myth continues. Every week American newspapers and magazines report new responsibilities and new twists on previous responsibilities. Recently we learned that a state administrator's association monthly publication boldly and proudly reported that the California state treasurer aims to teach the value of money. Will this be another subject? Will it be added to existing curriculum? Regardless, the treasurer hoped that 250 schools would participate in this program in school year 1997–1998. At least once a month a representative from a participating bank visits each school to open savings accounts and accept deposits. We say this sounds very worthy, but what program will be shortchanged to make this accommodation? No legislation exists or is being proposed to reduce the curricula. It is another add-on. The state treasurer says students need to learn more about money and its origins. We agree. But the legislature just doesn't get it. This program, too, will take classroom time and something will have to give. A recent publication in California reported that twenty California school districts have incorporated character education into their schools' curriculums using the Community of Caring program. Its proponents assert that "the result of this approach is a reduction in teen pregnancy, a reduction in violence, a reduction in drug and alcohol use, improved attendance and better academic performance" (Leon, 1997). Society has problems and schools are thought to be the vehicles for delivering the cure.

The Reality

The reality is that excessive diversification is a death knell. Examples from history are profound. The great Roman general Anthony was superb. He protected Caesar, conquered new territories, and put people to work for the Roman Empire. He did everything a general could be expected to do, and he was a husband and father, too. But he got too big for his britches. He foolishly thought he could do more. He believed his prowess was so grand that in addition to leading the massive Roman military he could conduct extracurricular affairs. The ensuing romance with Cleopatra and the voyages across the Mediterranean Sea took much time—time away from his duties as general. We dare say it distracted his thinking. He argued that he needed the time for rest and relaxation, and he no doubt did. Everyone needs rest and relaxation. But he bit off too much. The romance distracted him, he indulged his base desires, and he lost the focus and discipline that made him great—generaling. He essentially overdiversified, and it was his downfall.

Industry offers many examples, too. Business gurus Peters and Waterman (1982) coined a term—"stick to your knitting"—to illustrate that it is imperative to do what we do best and not get stretched too thin. W. Edwards Deming (1986) spoke of constancy of purpose to warn against overdiversification. Deming shared this and many other lessons with the Japanese, and they used it to win huge market shares in the global automobile, copying, and watch industries. One of us got wind of this lesson in 1982 while listening to the radio on a drive to a school in his district. It was a rendition of the catchy, old Human Benz tune, "Nobody but Me." The following is an excerpt from Mita's version: "No! No! No!

No! No! No! No! We don't make TVs—like they do; we don't make cameras—like they do; we don't make microwaves—like they do; we don't make vacuum cleaners—like they do. We make copiers, just copiers, just copiers, just copiers." Simple as that. The Japanese industries stuck to their knitting and literally beat up many American industries. Xerox, IBM, the automotive industry, Harley-Davidson, and others nearly went out of business. Finally, America learned and fought back with the same tactics. The late General Tire Corporation, too, offered an example of the disaster that can come from overdiversifying. Unfortunately, it learned too late and found itself operating destination resorts and making golf balls in the Southwest and sundry other products across the nation. In its last days it was not even making tires. That's real loss of focus. They lost it and failed to define a new one.

The same lesson applies to America's schools. They cannot do it all, nor can they do everything society wants and needs. We believe that America's public schools can do what they were intended to do, for example, teach children basic academic subjects and fine arts. Success would be second to none. Think about it. These are what administrators and teachers are trained to do, and doing it well takes time. Conducting self-esteem enhancement courses, piloting various curricula for public agencies, allowing service groups to erode school time to make noncurriculum-related presentations to students, providing food preparation services, operating bus transportation services, and the many efforts to arrest and eliminate gender, racial, and sexual orientation biases require schools to overdiversify and water down the curriculum. The original purpose of American schooling became secondary.[2]

The need to focus on learning is widely recognized. A report from the Committee for Economic Development (1994) states that "instead of focusing on what is most essential—improving learning and achievement—our society has turned the schools into social, ideological, and financial battlegrounds." The Public Agenda Foundation (1994) found that many of the schools' efforts are out of sync with what the public wants. The foundation found that the public believes that drugs and violence are the most serious threats. The second most serious threat to education was low academic standards and lack of emphasis on the basics. Eighty-nine percent of the public said that students should not graduate until they can write and speak English well. Ninety-two percent of African American parents, 87 percent of white parents, and 82 percent of the general public said that clear guidelines are needed on what kids should learn and teachers should teach in every major subject so that the kids and the teachers will know what to aim for. The 1994 report by the Committee for Economic Development says that those who govern and manage U.S. education are overwhelming the schools with conflicting demands that are more social than academic in nature. The report agrees with our contention that these conflicting demands have thwarted many years of educational reform. From a slightly different perspective, James Traub (2000) contends that the real problems lie with society, not with the schools.

Some of our colleagues argue that the social services that schools have assumed over the years are now so entrenched that eliminating them would be impossible—so we shouldn't try. True, there is a constituency for every cause. Every special add-on to the school's mission has a corresponding pressure group of parents whose children benefit from a larger share of the school's resources. Naturally, the groups that receive the most disproportionately large shares are the ones that apply the most intense political pressure—the squeakiest wheels. The answer, say our earnest colleagues, is to "collaborate" with other agencies so schools don't wind up doing it all. Most of these critics received their professional preparation in the schools-can-do-it-all era, and they feel that the myriad social tasks now assigned to educators are legitimate parts of the public school mission. "All we need is a little help." Unfortunately, help, in the form of collaboration with other public agencies or the private sector, never arrives. After all, what organization wants to take resources from its primary mission to be accountable for good driving habits or safe sex or emotional adjustment or racial desegregation? Give it to the schools, and it won't cost anything, right? Wrong. Every time something has been added, something has been lost.

A wise veteran superintendent tells of moving to a small, central California town to assume his first superintendency and asking a drywall contractor living next door to do a small remodeling job. Without hesitating, the contractor declined with an insightful justification. He explained, "I've been very successful in the new-construction drywall business. Years ago I learned that small remodel jobs may seem lucrative, but they take my concentration off my main job. When that happens, I become less successful at my primary business. I can't let that happen. Sorry." The new superintendent recognized the old contractor's wisdom and replied, "I hope you run for the school board. It seems that all we do in schools these days is 'small remodel jobs.' "

We believed so strongly in sticking to your knitting that we did not build a school with a full-service kitchen. As soon as we became superintendents we sold the buses to a company and hired it to provide transportation services. We refused to take time from the school day for the sundry checks the county medical agency demanded. If the service was needed, it could provide it before or after, but not during, school. Such encroachment would reduce the amount of time teachers can teach and improve productivity (see Chapter 8 for a discussion of the impact on learning when learning time is reduced). When seeking board approval to make these changes, the members asked, "Why?" The answer was easy. "The goal you defined for this district is academic and fine arts achievement, and you hired us, educators, to deliver it. That is what we've had success doing and frankly, we never took a course on bus transportation or food preparation." Borrowing from Mita, we said, "We don't do food preparation, we don't do transportation, etc., etc. No, we do school superintending. We know how to produce learning."

The point is that producing high-quality learning takes time and high-quality teaching. The other duties distract from these. But they are important. We would never say that breakfast and lunch, medical checks, counseling, or any of the other programs are unimportant. They are very important, and some other agency, or even the family, can perform them. We say that schools do not have the time, skill sets, or resources to do them and still produce the learning that America expects and needs. Countries that outscore us on achievement tests do not allow all of these things in their schools. They devote the school day to teaching *and learning*; they stick to their knitting.[3]

The Solution

The solution is clear.

First, school superintendents and school boards must be honest and admit that they cannot do it all. They must stand up and refuse to be a doormat for every agency and interest group that wants a chunk of the school day.

Second, schools; national, state, and local governments; churches; and other social agencies must publicly claim that education can never be optimized, or even good in some cases, without the *active involvement of the parents*. This dazzling flash of the obvious is voiced by many people. Pediatrician Perri Klass (1998), referring to her practice; a new book by Harris (1998); and a national study (Riley, 1996); reiterate the *flash* by stating that parenting practices, such as reading to children and having books in the home, have positive impacts on the children's readiness and desire to read. The importance of the family is voiced by the Pope, the Committee on Economic Development, public surveys, and yes, even recent presidents. Recently, thirty-three religious leaders put aside theoretical differences to join Secretary of Education Richard Riley in presenting a "Statement of Common Purpose" (Johnson, 1995). The document said that it is imperative that church communities join government, business, parents, and schools in helping all families participant in their children's education. The document concluded by saying that the religious community must play a more active and positive role in helping parents educate their children. In summary, "many school failures have little to do with what happens at school and a great deal to do with what happens (or fails to happen) at home. For the youngsters who come to school ready for learning, the schools are working pretty well" (Raspberry, 1992).

But getting the students to attend is also requisite to learning. In Detroit, 63,000 of the 180,000 public school students missed more than a month's worth of classes in the school year 1998–1999. That's one-ninth of the school year—gone! It is no mystery why learning is down in most inner-city schools. The nation is waking up. States are beginning to aggressively enforce laws that allow judges to punish truants' parents. In Brewton, Alabama, in May 1999 a grand jury indicted ten parents on misdemeanor charges punishable by up ninety 90 days in jail and a $100 fine. Similar penalties are being issued in Illinois and other states (Meredith, 1999).

Third, school boards must adopt key purposes of their districts and not deviate from them. They must direct the superintendents to deliver and measure their effectiveness on results (see Chapter 4 regarding board roles). No new programs will be added to the schools except those designed to better achieve the district's schools' designated purposes. When school board members learn of exciting new programs, approach the superintendent with great enthusiasm, and say "Let's do this!" the superintendents must compare the request to the board adopted purposes. If it is not a match, superintendents must say no and explain why.

A friend of ours summed this up with a story about his father and the one-pound sugar sack metaphor. While earning money during his summers as a youth, our friend put too much mortar on his father's mortarboard. It tipped over, spilled mortar all over the scaffolding, and created a mess. With relative calm, the father said, "Boy! you can't put two pounds of sugar in a one pound sack." The point, obviously, is that schools cannot continue to accept the social problems of the day and expect to teach the basics. Schools cannot do it all.

Notes

1. For a thorough review of the purposes of education, see Brubacher (1966), chapters 1, 3, 9, and 10. Also see L. Cremin (1980), introduction, chapter 1; and Cubberley (1948), *The History of Education*, Cambridge: The Riverside Press, chapter 20. Also see Myth 7 regarding values.

2. This does not imply that only the so-called *hard* should be taught. For an interesting discussion of *hard* and *soft* subjects and the need to teach the soft subjects, see Carnevale (1998). Also see chapter 7 regarding values.

3. For thorough discussion and presentation of data regarding this topic and the Third International Mathematics and Sciences Study (TIMSS) results, see Peak (1997); Schmidt (1996), and Stigler (1997).

References

Bridge, R. G., Judd, and Moock. (1979). *The Determinants of Educational Outcomes: The Impact of Families, Peers, Teachers and Schools.* Cambridge: Ballinger Press.

Brubacher, J. (1966). *A History of the Problems of Education.* New York: Mcgraw-Hill.

Carnevale, A. (1998). *Education for What? The New Office Economy.* Princeton: Educational Testing Service.

Coleman, J., et al. (1965). *Equality of Educational Opportunity.* Washington, DC: U.S. Department of Health, Education, and Welfare, Office of Education, U.S. Government Printing Office.

Committee for Economic Development. (1994). *Putting First Things First: Governing and Managing the Schools for High Achievement.* New York: Committee for Economic Development.

Cremin, L. (1980). *American Education: The Metropolitan Experience, 1876–1980.* New York: Harper and Row.

Cremin, L. (1980). *American Education: The National Experience, 1783–1876.* San Francisco: Harper Torchbooks.

Cubberley, E. (1948). *The History of Education.* Cambridge: Riverside Press.

Deming, W. (1986). *Out of the Crisis.* Cambridge: Massachusetts Institute of Technology, Center for Advanced Engineering Study.

Harris, J. (1998). *The Nurture Assumption: Why Children Turn Out the Way They Do.* New York: Free Press.

Johnston, R. (1995). "33 Religious Groups Join Riley in Seeking Greater Family Role in Schools, Leadership." Arlington, VA: American Association of School Administrators, p. 19.

Klass, P. (1998). "Even Now, Parents Really Do Matter." *San Diego Union-Tribune,* September 10, p. B11.

Leon, R. (1997). "The Community of Caring Comes to California." *The Social Studies Review: Journal of the California Council for the Social Studies.* (Vol. 37), pp. 73–74.

Meredith, R. (1999). "Truants' Parents Face Crackdown across the U.S." *New York Times* (vol. 149, no. 51,728), p. A1.

Peak, L. (1997). *Pursuing Excellence: A Study of U.S. Fourth Grade Mathematics and Science Achievement in International Context.* Washington, DC: National Center for Education Statistics, Office of Educational Research and Improvement, U.S. Department of Education.

Peters, T., and R. Waterman. (1982). *In Search of Excellence.* New York: Warner Books.

Public Agenda Foundation. (1994). "First Things First: What Americans Expect from the Public Schools."

Raspberry, W. (1992). "Despite Critics, Our Schools Work." *San Diego Union-Tribune*, February 21, section B, Opinion Page.

Raspberry, W. (1999). "Standards Won't Make Children Equal." *New York Times*, September 25, p. A32.

Riley R. (1996). *Reading Literacy in the United States*. Washington, DC: U.S. Department of Education, National Center for Education Statistics.

Schmidt, W. (1996). *Characterizing Pedagogical Flow: An Investigation of Mathematics and Science Teaching in Six Countries*. Bingham, MA: Kluwer.

Stigler, V. (1997). *The TIMSS Videotape Classroom Study: Methods and Preliminary Findings*. Olympus School District: office of Educational Research and Improvement, U.S. Department of Education.

Traub, J. (2000). "What No School Can Do." *New York Times Magazine*. (Vol. 149. no. 51, 269), p. 52.

Weissglass, J. (1998). "The SAT: Public-Spirited or Preserving the Privilege?" *Education Week* 17:31 (April 15), p. 60.

I TOOK AN I.Q. TEST...
AND THE RESULTS WERE NEGATIVE!?!

Introduction

Nearly two decades ago, President Reagan's *Nation at Risk* treatise raised the specter of our democracy being conquered by an evil empire because of its failure to keep pace with foreign competitors. Very soon, "accountability" became the battle cry. Frantically searching for ways to fix their schools, states throughout the union rushed to adopt punitive accountability laws. In many cases elaborate statewide testing programs were installed, with harsh political consequences for schools that failed to measure up. Unfortunately, the design and intent of those ventures failed to heed the warnings of savvy observers of school organizations. A decade of teaching to the tests proved fruitless. Once again, as we enter the twenty-first century, our political leaders are boarding the national standards and tests bandwagon, proclaiming this will finally fix the schools. It won't. And like the fear-based proposals of the past, it will probably do more harm than good.

At the core of this fad is a discredited "carrot and stick" behaviorist notion of accountability. When the man on the street talks about accountability in education these days, he usually means blame. To most of our political and business leaders, "standing accountable" does not mean taking responsibility in a collaborative enterprise aimed at achieving high quality. Rather, it means designating a person to take the blame if the enterprise falls short of its goals. In this behaviorist model of doing business, all but the top managers strive to keep goals from being "unreasonably high." All the rest of the organizational minions strive to keep production efforts focused narrowly on low-risk means to accomplish *immediate, short-term* results. "CYA" is the smart approach. Innovation and personal initiative are discouraged. In the school setting this translates to "teaching the test" instead of teaching *to* tests and the full curriculum. In business, this same mentality has helped to keep many American companies focused on short-term profit instead of long-range planning, which in turn stymied efforts to retool and improve production techniques. It is precisely this mentality that threatens to derail once again the school reform movement.

By 1998, thirty-two states and forty-three large urban school districts had adopted so-called accountability systems predicated on student testing. We agree with Al Ramirez's (November, 1999) contention that the drive toward high-stakes testing has the potential to become one of the major reform efforts of the century, "perhaps equal in impact to such movements as the development of the comprehensive high school or the racial integration of public education" (p. 205).

The unmistakable purpose of the current national goals, standards, and testing binge is to catch imaginary culprits, root out suspected incompetents, and place blame. A national goals, standards, and testing program of the sort currently being bandied about by fear-mongering politicians will not be the panacea the public hopes for. It will be just the opposite. It will misdirect the public schooling effort by leading it down the same path that some of our major industries took forty years ago when they paid more attention to short-term profits than to quality products.

Before we go farther, we want to make it clear that we are solidly in favor of rigorous testing and high standards. Colleagues who worked with us in the field through the years know we promote regular student and program testing and feedback at every grade level and in every subject several times per year. We believe that tests and standards that challenge students to excellent performance and provide educators with data to continuously improve instruction make good sense. But we are just as solidly opposed to the typical standardized testing again being proposed. These tests rarely challenge any of our students. If you doubt this, ask them! And if the question is simply how our students are doing, then far less expensive and decidedly less intrusive samplings are certainly sufficient.

Why, then, do the politicians keep coming back to this simplistic formula for school reform? We believe it is simply part of a proven, but not terribly prudent, ploy to gather followers by capitalizing on the American public's firmly established fear of losing its position of dominance in the world. This fear has been a driving force in U.S. politics for decades. In the 1950s Admiral Hyman Rickover warned that the Soviet Union would soon bury or at least surpass U.S. technologically unless we radically reformed the nation's school curriculum. Rickover's pronouncements in combination with Sputnik helped lead a panicky Congress to pass the National Defense Education Act. Using large federal grants as incentives, the federal government began a national reform effort aimed at developing a new math and a new science to keep up with the Russians. As we mention in our discussion of school size, the United States recaptured the lead in space in an astonishingly short time—ironically, with scientists and engineers trained in the supposedly outdated science and math, while the first young graduates of the *new* math and science were having trouble balancing their checkbooks.

The Myth

Proponents of national goals, standards, and tests argue correctly that the impact of accountability lies in its power to focus attention on what is important. They say this can be accomplished only when the goals and standards are specified. Schools in the United States have had educational goals for more than a century, but they've been vague and general. The testing proponents point out that we have not developed a system to let us know if we are reaching those goals. Since specific, measurable targets have not been set, we don't know how far we are from where we want to be, or the rate of our progress. Our assessment and testing programs indicate only whether we are making progress or losing ground. National standards, they argue, would establish benchmarks, and common agreement could be established on what students should know and be able to do when they move from grade to grade or graduate from high school.

Proponents continue by claiming that schools could then develop clear and understandable ways of communicating progress. Data on the percentage of students who have mastered number facts when they exit the first grade could be reported and tracked from year to year. Likewise, reading, language arts, math, science, and other important skills could be compiled on graduating seniors. Educators usually agree that "you get what you test." An assessment program drives curriculum, focusing instruction on those aspects of student performance that are most essential. In addition to informing the public about the progress of student achievement, testing programs also inform the faculties about the strengths and weaknesses in student performance and provide the feedback essential to constant improvement of the instructional program.

The national test boosters explain that building goals and standards around the agreed-upon outcomes of education should be fairly simple. The American Society for Training and Development and the U.S. Department of Labor, Employment, and Training Administration, for example, have listed seven skill groups considered to be workplace "basics."[1] They are as follows:

- Learning to learn—the ability to absorb, process, and apply information quickly and effectively;
- Listening and oral communication;
- Competence in reading, writing, and computation—including additional proficiency in summarizing information, monitoring one's own work, and using analytical and critical thinking skills;
- Adaptability—creative thinking and problem solving;
- Personal management—self-esteem, goal setting, motivation, and personal/career development—taking pride in work accomplished, setting goals and meeting them, and enhancing job skills to meet new challenges;
- Group effectiveness—interpersonal skills, negotiation, and teamwork; and
- Organizational effectiveness and leadership—a sense of where the

organization is headed and what it must do to make a contribution—an ability to assume responsibility and motivate coworkers.

Clearly these skill groups require instruction that fosters critical thinking and problem solving in the classroom. And in the classroom, on a daily, weekly, semester, and yearly basis, we agree that these skill groups can be regularly and comprehensively tested. But can this be done on a national basis with a test once per year or once every three years? Will we be able to reduce our dropout rate, improve scores on international achievement tests, or cure adult illiteracy by imposing national tests?

Conclusion? **The Reality**

Americans have a reverent and unswerving faith in tests. The hard truth is that testing instruments fall far short of the mark in measuring the types of student performance that really count. They simply don't measure what Americans think they measure and neither does the IQ test score contemplated by the forlorn student in the cartoon at the beginning of this chapter. Those of us who have extensive experience in raising scores know that state tests demand that a school's curriculum be "comprehensive," meaning it must cover a *broad* range of subject matter. Unfortunately, teachers can't spend precious time delving into every area (or even a few areas) in depth, for fear their classes won't be properly prepared for the test. So they "cover" as much as possible—but thinly. Ted and Nancy Sizer (November, 1999) are right on target when they assert that teachers who emphasize preparation for a machine-graded test are missing the boat. "Those teachers (and the principals and parents flogging them to get the test scores up) are neglecting an important part of the [learning] process" (p. 190). We won't spend time discussing how forcing teachers into this predicament thwarts their efforts to create high-level thinkers and learners, but we believe that the omnipresent standardized tests have shaped an American public school curriculum that the Third International Mathematics and Sciences Study (TIMSS) researchers (Schmidt, 1996) quite appropriately compare to "an acre of water an inch deep." Japan and Germany both spend *more* time on *less* subject matter than does the United States. And, yes, they test students rigorously. The difference is they do not test for the purpose of comparing one student with another or one school with another school.

In spite of significant efforts at the state and local levels, most new and revised standardized testing programs implemented so far have not materially supported education reform. In fact, for the most part, these tests actually obstruct progress. True, testing to provide feedback is an essential component of an instructional program and is powerfully effective when designed properly and used for this purpose. But testing can also be used as a supervision strategy—a sort of performance inspection or surveillance. The purpose of the testing and the way it is carried out shape the teachers' response. Will the teachers teach for depth of understanding, creative thinking, problem solving and application, or will the teachers spend long hours practicing the test format and drilling the students on district-prepared materials designed to score well on the assessment instruments? Will the teachers promote creative classroom experiences and use the test data as indicators for instructional improvement, or will the teachers narrowly focus on tested content and view the test results as a measure of teaching performance? Will it be rich, creative teaching? Or CYA? Unfortunately, we know the answers to these questions.

Oppressive supervision suppresses teacher creativity and autonomy. It spawns organizational friction and squelches productivity. The same can be said of state and national testing programs aimed at establishing the popular notion of accountability. As we said previously, a comprehensive testing program properly conceived is a powerful, positive influence on a school system's curriculum planning and development. It can be a way for teachers to monitor their progress in order to improve their instruction, their curriculum, and, most important, the performance of their students. But a program perceived to be administrative surveillance of teachers or schools spells disaster.

Organizational accountability built around the understanding and belief that human beings are born with a natural desire to be productive results in an explosion of human energy. In these settings, national standards might be valuable as means to establish direction, to help identify weaknesses, and to inspire improved instruction. In the hands of the local schools and faculties, standards and tests could help lead our schools to higher levels of performance. Still, standards and tests used to coerce educators by assigning blame and threatening various sanctions will have a very predictable response. Only this time, with one national institution or even one big national committee deciding what our children should be taught and how they should be tested, the results will be far more disastrous than the long list of failed state experiments of the past half-century.

More than forty-five years ago the American statistician W. Edwards Deming rejected behaviorism as a means to motivate organizations. Instead he developed beliefs and strategies more in line with Maslow's hierarchy of needs and the human relations organizational theories being developed during that period. It is pure irony that Deming's strategies were adopted by postwar Japan and helped to transform that once-devastated nation into a world model of productivity, quality, and industrial excellence (Deming, 1986). The ideas that nourished Japan's modern industrial juggernaut are getting more play today in the United States, but they still have not been accepted widely by our business, industrial, political, and, yes, educational leaders. And it's no wonder. Most of these leaders are products of American schools. They are steeped in what may be America's tragic flaw—the pervasive behaviorist idea that people are best motivated by pain or pleasure.

Attempts to Cope with the Myth

Most educators long ago conceded that accountability by testing is, for the foreseeable future, our way of life in American schools. And most recognize that it seems to make good sense to the man on the street. Taxpayers have a right to know how their investment is faring. It is up to the professional educators to do it right—to design and implement effective accountability measures that do not impede teaching and learning. Early in the 1990s, California's educational leaders recognized that the curriculum frameworks produced by the California Department of Education called for instruction that empowers students, but the narrow scope of the state's assessment program did not support that instruction. They correctly determined that the statewide testing program that had been in place since the 1970s did not challenge students to think and did not encourage teachers to foster critical thinking or productive problem solving in the classroom. Typical of most mass-testing programs, the old tests did not sample the powerful outcomes specified in the frameworks. Instead, they focused on more trivial and *easily measured* results. Most of the tests used a multiple choice format for reasons of efficiency and economy. Besides, widely held theories of the day postulated that complex skills and understanding could be judged by sampling discrete subskills and bits of information. The result of more sophisticated thinking was a shift in the statewide assessment program to greater emphasis on direct writing assessment, open-ended questions in mathematics, and an attempt to develop hands-on science assessment. These attempts to install so-called authentic assessment were meant to repair some of the aspects of the old assessment program that were most damaging to student learning. The idea behind the authentic testing methodologies is that the task is large enough and significant enough to warrant teachers and students focusing their efforts on it and practicing it. In other words, make the test comprehensive enough so that teaching to the test will be a valuable learning experience. An authentic test, such as writing an essay, is worth practicing. We agree.

Naturally, these authentic methods of testing are far more expensive than the economical, machine-scored bubble tests. The cost of scoring thousands of essays far exceeds the cost of electronic scanning and scoring, and the tests themselves are subject to suspicion and criticism. Moreover, standardized scores on essays for the purpose of comparisons are far less reliable than the old standby, the multiple-choice format.

Sadly, most Americans still foolishly believe in the magic of the standardized test and demand that their tax dollars go to support "above-average" schools. It should have been no surprise when the Friends of Education survey of all fifty states found *that no state was below average* at the elementary level on any of the six major nationally known, commercially available tests. It doesn't take much imagination to figure out what happened. As soon as the tests are published, school districts begin to narrow their curricula and instruction to focus on the areas tested. Tests are analyzed, and students are drilled in the testing format. Publishers claim that they can revise and renorm the tests only every six to ten years. Consequently, the scores reported to the public from tests of this sort are mostly fraudulent. When you consider that national surveys (such as the ones conducted by the Center for Research and Evaluation, Standards, and Student Testing at UCLA) have indicated that neither teachers nor administrators actually *use* standardized test results, the practice of statewide testing taking place around the country begins to look like a monumental financial fiasco. The results are not credible or useful, and in many cases they hinder the teaching and learning processes. To compound this sorry state of affairs by imposing a national testing program on the nation's schools would be at best an enormous waste of money. Clearly the concept of accountability testing must be drastically reformed to eliminate the mortal defects and to accomplish what an assessment program is supposed to do.

Recommendations

Any national test must be simply one component of a larger, more comprehensive testing system that authentically and meaningfully assesses local performance standards. This makes a lot more sense than one federal agency determining what our children should learn and what our teachers should teach. The responsibility must be shared. A comprehensive system should encourage local schools to assess student performance in every classroom at every grade level at great depth. A program of this sort should be mandatory for every school district in the country, but it must be locally owned and operated. The American tradition of local control, as well as the apparent folly of highly centralized educational operations, demands a focus at the local level—with instruments developed by local faculty directed by and in consultation with testing experts. The state and federal role should be one of leadership, that is, they should develop testing frameworks and guidelines, provide training for local school districts, and monitor test administration.

To succeed, a national testing program (and state programs, for that matter) must drop school-by-school, district-by-district scores and rankings. The most insidious aspect of a testing program is the practice of publishing scores by school and by district. Releasing the data by region would accomplish the mission of measuring the public school efforts without corrupting instruction and without encouraging the practice of teaching the tests. (Note once again that we make a distinction between "teaching the test," an improper classroom strategy aimed at boosting scores at all costs, and "teaching *to* tests," a logical and proper classroom strategy.) School-by-school, classroom-by-classroom growth and improvement could then be encouraged by comprehensive, locally tailored assessment devices that are used to diagnose and prescribe rather than to compare and rank. These would allow faculties to determine how well they are accomplishing what they set out to accomplish without feeling compelled to teach the test to artificially boost school or classroom ratings.

If the federal government and states were sincere about radically improved education, they would demand that a strong assessment system driven by the local curriculum be developed in every district with the support of the state. Conversely, they would not impose a centrally developed standardized test. The powerful benefits of integrating well-developed curriculum with comprehensive, authentic, criterion-referenced testing have been demonstrated (Glatthorn, 1997; Moss-Mitchell, 1998). But the purposes of the testing must be diagnosis and improvement, not ranking and rating. A proper sampling of the state or even various regions would produce data for the taxpayer without the bitter consequences of the proposed statewide or national tests administered to every student and reported in a way that compares schools and districts.

Most states require school districts to contract for a financial management audit every year. States serious about the delivery of curriculum and instruction could require a curriculum management audit at least every two years. Regular state-mandated audits of curriculum and instructional programs combined with quality requirements and strong technical support would reap enormous benefits. Phi Delta Kappa, for example, sponsors a sophisticated curriculum management auditing process that could be replicated immediately with minimum costs.[2] Instead of embarking upon the establishment of massive state-run curriculum assessment and supervision systems, state governments could assume leadership and support roles and above all demand that each local school system's instructional program be well managed, internally consistent, organizationally sound, and *truly* accountable.

Finally, the national and state Departments of Education could reorganize to emphasize accountability defined as *responsibility*, not *blame*. This chapter's appendix describes some of the appropriate roles of federal and state governments in support of local school district efforts.

Under this proposal, states would not only develop curriculum frameworks but assessment frameworks as well. These frameworks or guidelines would require that specific outcomes be assessed and certain testing methods be used. The framework would also specify the extent to which each separate content area of the curriculum would be tested as well as the nature and quality of the scores. The federal government would spend its time with the identification of national priorities as well as the support of research and development. In addition, they would coordinate with states for the collection, analysis, and dissemination of nationwide data.

Instead of being burdened heavily with the nuts and bolts of administering competency tests to every student in the state, a state department of education would spend its time and resources conducting ongoing research and development that would result in improved structures for objective measurement and new techniques to evaluate student performance. For a fraction of the cost of the current system, the department could develop and refine authentic, performance-based assessment technologies and train district staffs to adapt them to local uses.

The department would also establish the technical criteria that local districts must meet in order for their assessments to be approved for use. These technical criteria would include standards for test validity and reliability, as well interpretability. Data would be actually used for curriculum decision making—in the classroom, by the principal, at the district level, and by the school board. Finally, and probably most important, the state's department of education would certify curriculum auditors. Using the modified version of the financial model now used throughout the nation, districts would be required to contract with certified curriculum auditors on a regular basis. The long-sought-after school "accountability" would be achieved in a meaningful, healthy manner.

Notes

1. The 1988 report of the American Society for Training and Development and the U.S. Department of Labor, Employment, and Training Administration, entitled *Workplace Basics: The Skills Employers Want*, specifies the skills graduates need as identified by the business community. This report was one of the foundations for a discussion paper, entitled *Educational Assessment: Harnessing the Power of Information to Improve Student Performance*, used at the 1989 California Education Summit and included in the summit's final report available from the California

Department of Education. Workplace basics are reviewed in the section entitled "The Testing Reform We Really Need."

2. Curriculum audits are described in detail in *The Curriculum Management Audit*, edited by Larry Frase, Fenwick English, and Bill Poston (1994). This is a thorough description of the curriculum auditing process developed originally by Fenwick English and currently sponsored by Phi Delta Kappa. Curriculum audits are also sponsored by two state affiliates—The Association of California School Administrators (Burlingame, California) and the Texas Education Agency (Austin, Texas).

References

Deming, W. E. (1986). *Out of the Crisis*. Cambridge: MIT Center for Advanced Engineering Study.

Glatthorn, A. (1997). *The Principal as Curriculum Leader*. Thousand Oaks, CA: Corwin Press.

Moss-Mitchell, F. (1998). "The Effects of Curriculum Alignment on the Mathematics Achievement of Third-grade Students as Measured by the Iowa Tests of Basic Skills: Implications for Educational Administrators." Unpublished dissertation, Clark Atlanta University, Atlanta, Georgia.

Ramirez, A. (1999). "Assessment-Driven Reform—The Emperor Still Has No Clothes." *Phi Delta Kappan* 81(3) (November).

Resnick, L, and J. Wirt, eds. (1996). *Linking School and Work: Roles for Standards and Assessment*. San Francisco: Jossey-Bass Publishers.

Schmidt, W., et al. (1996). *A Splintered Vision: An Investigation of U.S. School Mathematics and Science Education*. The Third International Mathematics and Sciences Study (TIMSS), National Science Foundation News.

Sizer, T., and N. Sizer (1999). "Grappling." *Phi Delta Kappan* 81(3) (November).

Appendix
National, State, and Local Roles in a Comprehensive Testing Program

National	State	Local
Identification of national priorities and standards	Development of curriculum and assessment frameworks	Identification of local performance
Support of research and development	Research and development on curriculum and assessment strategies	Development of assessment instruments
Nationwide data collection, analysis, and reporting	Staff-development training for local district staff-development personnel	Administration of assessment at every grade level and of every student
	Certification of curriculum auditors	Diagnosis of test data for curriculum decision making and instructional improvement

MYTH 3:
TEACHER UNIONS HAVE HELPED
TEACHERS AND EDUCATION

Introduction

After more than three decades of unionized teachers across the United States, two predominant questions have emerged: Have unions helped teachers? Have unions helped education? In 1993, *Forbes* magazine noted that the rise of teacher unions in America coincided with skyrocketing costs and apparently deteriorating performance (Brimlow and Spencer, 1993). Although no cause-and-effect relationship was claimed, the authors made a good case that today's big teacher unions are giving us less for more. These criticisms strike a responsive chord among many parents and educators who are increasingly convinced that teacher unions and their questionable tactics share a large part of the blame for the shabby condition of our public school system and especially the declining prestige of the teaching profession.

Unionization of taxpayer-supported enterprises has historically been viewed skeptically by political scientists and economists. After all, the ultimate tool in the union arsenal is a strike, designed to put the enterprise out of business if a satisfactory agreement cannot be negotiated. The Teamsters strike against United Parcel Service (UPS) in 1997 had all the classic characteristics of an industrial-era strike—including the threat to UPS of diminishing the market share and the threat to the Teamsters of lost jobs. Both occurred. But life for most of us returned to normal very quickly. After all, nobody really cares whether UPS retains its preeminent position in the package delivery world or whether the drivers are financially strapped for a few months—except, perhaps, the owners of the company and the families of the drivers. But the welfare of our country and our children is quite a different matter altogether.

Why would a government establish self-destructive mechanisms like this, especially in an enterprise as fundamental to a democracy's survival as public education? Allowing public servants to withhold essential services in order to gain leverage on the taxpayers at the bargaining table was unequivocally rejected by such labor union champions as Franklin D. Roosevelt and George Meany. FDR's administration sponsored the National Labor Relations Act, granting formal governmental sanction to labor unions throughout the nation, and George Meany was the powerful president of the AFL-CIO—both strong advocates of organized labor in the private sector. Yet both men felt that unions in the public sector would lead to unacceptable abuse. Modern-day supporters of teacher unionism, of course, feel otherwise.

We don't deny that unions played a major role in improving the life of Americans toiling in the coal mines and sweatshops during the first half of the twentieth century. Thanks to the political muscle of unions and to enlightened management philosophies, most of America's industries have abandoned the labor practices that spawned the union movement in the first place. However, in more recent years changes in technology have radically altered the nature of the workplace and the worker. Knowledge and the manipulation of information have become as important as capital, real estate, and labor. This, combined with labor-saving robotics, has led to a dramatic change in the composition of the labor force. Researchers, health care professionals, computer scientists, and teachers lead the knowledge revolution, and these occupations clearly are not compatible with the traditional industrial labor model. None of us are surprised that all this has led to a plunge in union membership in the private sector. The result has been a healthy movement toward organizations that inspire higher levels of productivity from their members. How then can unionization possibly benefit education?

The Myth

Unionists are convinced that school board members and administrators view teachers as hired help, not equal partners in the educational enterprise. They claim that the medieval class barriers between administrators and teachers must be broken down before school district organizations can function using modern principles of organizational management. In other words, school districts can become democratic organizations only when all participants are considered *equals*, not masters and servants. In the long run, according to the union bosses, this is what collective bargaining can accomplish: a progression from a master-servant chain of command to a democratic organization—like a child who first accepts his father's protection and domination, then rebels, and finally assumes his rightful position as a full partner in the family.

Teacher unions promise to achieve for their members the equality of status necessary for a higher functioning, democratic profession, as well as the bread-and-butter issues of more money, more benefits, less hours, better working conditions, and so forth. Depending upon the mix of personalities involved in the school district, the progression from "infancy" to "adulthood" can be filled with conflict and violence, or it can be relatively peaceful. The late Al Shanker (Woo, 1996), the longtime president of the American Federation of Teachers (AFT), once proposed that the progression might entail "blowing up" the districts. But regardless of the nature of the transition, a mature labor-management relationship cannot materialize in a school district without substantial changes in the attitudes among the school boards and administrators—and this, according to the unionists, can only be accomplished by the intervention of a powerful union.

Ken Parker, a leading teacher-union bargaining specialist and a veteran of school district labor wars from New York to California, describes the progression of labor relations from infancy to adulthood as a continuum (see Appendix to this chapter).

This seasoned union pro contends that the continuum begins with *paternalism*. Teachers and other school staff members enjoy a "father–son" relationship with administrators and supervisors, who provide for all employee needs and regulate employee conduct. The relationship is based on the authority of the administration and is totally conditioned upon the goodwill of individual administrators.

After President Kennedy's 1961 executive order allowing federal civil servants to unionize, many states installed collective bargaining plans for teachers, and the relationship with administrators in numerous districts changed radically to *enemy*. This phase of the continuum, which still exists in many "adolescent" districts in the nation, is characterized by a reluctance on the part of school district leaders to recognize the legitimate existence of unions, and by incessant threats and challenges made by union officials.

The enemy phase, according to Parker, eventually becomes less a hostile *adversary*, maintaining strong resistance and an arm's-length relationship. In this phase district leaders accept the legitimate existence of the union, and union leaders generally concede that district leaders need room to administer school programs effectively.

Parker goes on to explain that the adversary phase of the continuum often mellows further to *advocacy*. The district accepts the union and respects its rights and roles. Union leaders support and maintain their positions and proposals but do not challenge or threaten the district's leadership. This phase of the continuum represents a mature, workable arrangement that allows a traditional line-and-staff, master-servant type of organization to function with minimal abuse of teachers by administrators and minimal disruption of operations by teachers. It represents the farthest point to which a labor-management relationship can advance without major mutual concessions by the leadership of both factions.

The ultimate payoff on the continuum is, according to the bargaining specialists, *collaboration*. To achieve this ideal, the union must be willing to submerge the advocacy relationship to gain broad objectives beneficial to both the employees and the district. Likewise, the district must be willing to give up part of its authority to the employees who are accomplishing the mission of the school system. These are hard pills to swallow for both sides. But if the leaders can pull it off, problem solving instead of positional confrontation becomes the standard operating procedure for all matters of mutual concern to the district and its unions.

Once this magical homeostasis between the interests of management and labor has been achieved, say the backers of collective bargaining, the stage is set for the interests of teachers to be significantly advanced— including bread-and-butter issues of salary, benefits, and workload. A greater equality of status among the various occupations in a school system now would allow the best and the brightest to remain in teaching rather than in seeking administrative positions in order to augment their salaries. Moreover, the faculty would be safe from persecution by avaricious, politically motivated administrators. "All of this," proclaim the union leaders, "and cheap life insurance, too!"

Sounds good. And respected advocates like Ken Parker are very convincing. But after three decades of teacher unions, are we closer to this Shangri-La? In truth, only an insignificantly small fraction of districts in America has completed the journey to collaboration.

The Reality

Today's union-fomented school district turmoil, coupled with a popularly held perception of rapidly declining public school performance and escalating per-pupil expenditures, suggests that Roosevelt and Meany were right. Unionism in the public sector leads to unacceptable abuse. It can be argued that the decline in school performance has been greatly exaggerated and the escalation in costs has been largely a result of uncontrolled expansion in services to the special education population. However, the unions clearly have not kept their word to teachers. Teachers today are not better off financially as a result of industrial-style collective bargaining.

In the 1950s, the advent of Sputnik further emphasized the necessity of world-class education, especially the necessity of attracting the best and brightest into teaching. This caused Americans to focus their priorities on schools; coupled with the baby boom shortage of trained classroom personnel, this caused teacher salaries in real dollars to increase rapidly. Then came widespread unionization of teachers and promises of even more. However, in today's dollars, wages for teachers actually declined during the 1970s, the time when teacher unions were reaching a peak of influence. In fact, teachers today have still not achieved the spending power they had in the post-Sputnik era in spite of frantic union activity across the nation and enormous increases in union bureaucracies liberally sprinkled with executives pulling down six-figure salaries.[1] To make matters worse, our teachers have had to swallow significantly higher, and often mandatory, union dues to support these free-spending bureaucracies—giving them even fewer take-home dollars.

Tragically, the extended conflict within school districts caused by industrial-type labor relations during this period has denied teachers the full satisfaction of teaching with compensating advancement in their professional status or salaries. This was the unfortunate result of teacher unions using industrial-type strategies focused on working conditions, meaning the number of hours worked, the number of minutes allotted for breaks, criteria for leaves, penalties for tardiness, and so on. Administrators and their negotiators claimed to be preserving power for the elected school board, while union bosses claimed they were protecting the workers from the connivances of unscrupulous management. None of this promoted collaboration or joint efforts to accomplish mutually held goals. In fact, industrial union leaders of the "old school" counseled their local officers *not* to become involved in the governance of an organization. They reasoned that collaboration with management in governing the organization would compromise or "co-opt" them as effective advocates for and "protectors" of the "workers."

Unnecessary Union Protection

The role of the union as "protector" of teachers is ludicrous in the public school context. By the end of World War II, most states had passed extensive laws that guaranteed teachers everything from special free speech protection to strict due process for disciplinary matters and tenure. Moreover, state legislatures were becoming much more prescriptive about the working conditions of teachers and school employees. The states and the nation as a whole were beginning to realize that the continued position of the United States as a world leader demanded a guaranteed high-quality education immune from the whims of local school boards. As a result, by the mid-1960s, when the militant unionization of public employees exploded following Kennedy's executive order, most of the protections that private-sector unions had sought over the years were already enacted in state law, preempting the need for extensive industrial-style labor contracts. In addition, the courts ran in tandem with the legislatures in protecting teachers. For example, the U.S. Supreme Court blunted the ability of school boards arbitrarily to dismiss teachers who incurred their displeasure. Since the 1960s, the high court has protected teachers' rights to free speech and association and has defined the property and liberty interests of teachers that trigger due-process protections. These protections are guaranteed regardless of the existence of a negotiated contract.

What's more—our comments on school board myths notwithstanding—school trustees tend to be the best employers in town. School boards usually are composed of members who are more or less representative of the faction in the community most interested in children and education. If given a chance, they want to treat their employees fairly. However, they are also politicians, and they do not want to look stupid in the eyes of their constituents. When forced into a traditional negotiations mind-set, board members invariably feel that it is smarter to be hard-bargaining horse traders, in the finest Yankee tradition, than to join forces with the opposition to work out mutually acceptable plans. In stark contrast, these same board members will make "concessions" to employees without demanding the usual quid pro quo when the model is a collaborative one and the goal is to develop a higher quality school system. For example, one board in a California district practicing a collaborative labor relations model decided to allow teachers to take extended *paid* personal leave by allowing teachers to pay for their substitutes. Nothing was "demanded" in return. Board members simply were convinced that teachers given this professional latitude would not abuse it and that the result would be a more professional, more productive faculty—in other words, a higher quality educational system would result. They were right, but to board members faced with the industrial-style bargaining traditions, such an agreement would be pure lunacy.

Both District and Community Suffer

Formal industrial-style negotiations actually restrict and confuse communications in the school district. Although experienced negotiators would argue with the terminology, formal negotiations require dishonesty by both parties. For example, it is well established in National Labor Relations Board precedents that management cannot bring to the table a single "take-it-or-leave-it" offer. Rather, both parties are required to "move." In other words, a school board that has determined that the cost-of-living and income projections warrant a 7 percent salary increase must make a much smaller initial offer in order to leave room to move. Likewise, a teacher union that does a similar analysis will arrive at a similar bottom-line figure but must begin at a substantially higher position for the same reason.

The result is predictable: confusion, suspicion, and distrust. Teachers are confused and hurt when they hear that the school board is offering an unreasonably low cost-of-living raise in spite of the fact that the state has announced a substantial cost-of-living increase to the district. Conversely, board members and administrators are shocked at the teacher union's demands for an exorbitant salary increase with seemingly no regard for the enormous reduction in programs and student services that such an increase would require. The truth, of course, is that both sides are *lying*. Teachers don't want to strip the district of its programs, and the board members recognize fully the need to raise salaries to keep up with increasing costs. But both sides must begin with proposals far from reality to give them room to move. It is simply the way the game is played. Incredible as it might seem, lying is actually a *requirement* of the bargaining process—hardly conducive to the high levels of communication and collaboration characteristic of high-quality organizations.

To make matters worse, in order to play the game properly the union

must regularly discredit the vision and direction of the district's leadership. Otherwise, union leaders would face the difficult task of convincing
the staff and community that the management's wastefulness and insen-
sitivity is only a periodic occurrence that coincidentally happens when
the contract is being negotiated. Confounding communications in order
to cause staff members to be suspicious about their leadership also helps
the union maintain its traditional industrial role as job protector.

Probably most harmful to both teachers and school districts is the loss
of public confidence caused by combative industrial-style bargaining. Adversarial labor negotiations between a teacher union and a school board
seriously injure a district's fragile community relations. The credibility of
the school district's administration is shaken by labor turmoil, and respect for the teaching faculty is lowered. This stems from the fundamental difference between public-sector and private-sector unions.

The union's primary weapon is political power, not economic power.
The union knows the state will not shut down the school district, even if
it loses some of its students due to parent dissatisfaction. Consequently,
teacher leaders must put political pressure on the school board and administration in order to gain an advantage at the bargaining table. This
means "stirring up" the teachers and parents in the district by proclaiming the district to be "mismanaged" and accusing board members and
administrators of wasting taxpayer dollars on unimportant priorities.
Most of this, of course, is untrue, but it rallies the troops and dismays the
public. In this political battle for the minds of the voters, the district must
counter by pointing out that teachers are already well paid, and, based
on the fewer number of days they work, are actually far better paid than
most of the constituent taxpayers. This is also largely untrue, but it adds
balance to the propaganda war.

Over the years, we have noticed that the community, ironically, believes
both the union's attack rhetoric and the district's defense propaganda.
After the smoke has cleared and the contract is settled, the community is
more convinced than ever that its school district is governed by bungling,
insensitive administrators and that its classrooms are staffed with over-
paid and underworked teachers. Convincing parents that their children
are in competent hands becomes more and more difficult each year.
Today, comments that disparage public school teachers or minimize their
efforts are rarely challenged, even by school administrators, formerly the
staunchest defenders of teachers and the public school enterprise. In
short, adversarial union processes undermine the basis of community
support upon which a successful public school system depends. They
also drive an artificial wedge between school leaders, who by law must
be designated "management," and the unit member teachers, who by implication are relegated to worker status—hardly a desirable feature of a
high-quality, collaborative twenty-first-century organization.

The Solution

So far the union movement in public schools has helped neither teachers nor education. (See the cartoon, which pokes fun at union bosses and underscores a bitter reality.) Only union officials and a few administrators have a better life—at the expense of the rank-and-file teacher. We can do better. It is as simple as changing the laws that establish and define collective bargaining for teachers. Reform in education requires that we organize our schools to unleash the creativity and productivity of our teachers. This requires a system that deals with teachers as professionals, and it begins with collaborative employer-employee relationships. Teacher unions constitute a major part of the education system. No reform effort can be successful if it ignores reform in labor laws.

What would those reforms in education labor law look like? First, the legislatures must mandate sound communications structures within every district, with arbitration built in for union leaders or administrators who lag behind in comprehending the "new order" and with strong oversight responsibilities for the state's department of education. Any one of several structures that have been developed and successfully implemented will work. We prefer a joint union-management council at the highest administrative level with links to school site administrators, faculty, and staff (see Streshly and DeMitchell, 1994).

Second, lawmakers must recognize the wisdom of Meany and Roosevelt and outlaw teacher strikes. Teachers, like firefighters and police, assume a public trust and cannot be accorded unrestricted rights to disrupt operations of essential public services. Children in this country have a firmly established, constitutionally protected right to an appropriate education. Moreover, they have a similar established legal right to attend a safe, properly supervised school. It is patently irresponsible for state legislatures to permit union walkouts that abridge these rights and that have, in several instances, put children in mortal danger.

Third, the state governments must establish criteria for teacher salaries that require all districts to compensate faculty fairly and in a manner that recognizes merit. Although both unionists and legislators quake at the suggestion, statewide salary schedules and schemes for compensating teachers should be considered. The issue is fairness and equity in compensating teachers. Statewide salary schedules would allow state legislators to deal directly and honestly with teacher salaries, instead of resorting to complicated political manipulations of school district appropriations in the form of so-called categorical funds to prevent "too much" from being bargained away in local negotiations.

Fourth, legislatures must mandate professional standards for teachers that demand peer involvement in individual teacher performance, as well as school and district performance. High-quality organizations are those that promote the full potential of each constituent human being. This can be achieved only by enterprises that regard all roles and tasks as important and valuable, where all contributors are respected. But this organizational ideal cannot be achieved through the traditional master-servant relationships. Rather, the ideal is achieved by organizations that encourage all employees to dedicate themselves to continual enhancement of their organization's mission, including the enhancement of fellow-employee performance. The prime examples of these sorts of organizations are emerging as leaders in the world today, and the principles they employ are those advocated by American statistician W. Edwards Deming and a new generation of organizational quality gurus.[2]

The collective bargaining model adopted by teachers when they entered the bargaining arena four decades ago was the one that seemed at that time to be working for the industrial unions.

We now know that the adversarial model was failing there, too. Today, modern teacher union leaders, like their industrial-sector counterparts, are recognizing the need to build better labor-management relations. The American Federation of Teachers (AFT), once a militant, adversarial teacher union affiliated with the industrial-sector AFL-CIO, has led the way in efforts to establish collaborative labor relations with districts across the nation. More recently, the National Education Association (NEA), now merged with the AFT, took steps to clean up its unsavory popular image by supporting the practice of teachers reviewing their peers—once considered taboo by protection-oriented, industrial-style unions. The union president hailed this departure from industrial-style labor relations as "new unionism." Others saw it as a welcome return to the more reasonable practices of preunion days. But regardless of the historical perspective, we view this small step as a breakthrough. For collaborative school labor relations to work, both sides must take responsibility for excellence in the classroom. Certainly part of NEA's action was in response to the potential for losing further ground with legislators. Several state legislatures around the country are seriously reconsidering teacher tenure laws and other protections heretofore taken for granted by teachers. Lawmakers see little reason to put up with the headaches of big teacher unions while at the same time giving teachers the special status under the law they enjoyed in preunion days. Endorsing peer review blunts the arguments of the antitenure lobby and may help prevent another major loss to the teaching profession at the hands of the union. Regardless of the motives, however, the NEA's concession to the proponents of "new unionism" is a ray of sunshine for all public schools.

In the final analysis, though, the American people cannot expect teacher unions to perform the necessary surgery on themselves. Effective reform of teacher unions lies in the hands of the legislatures of each state. Procedures such as the ones outlined above must be put into law—and soon. These measures will encourage dialogue between management and unions and will discourage demagoguery on both sides of the table. Strikes must be outlawed by laws with teeth, and processes that impose outside settlement must be adopted for districts that lag behind in the development of mature protocols. Above all, the fighting and bickering must cease. Our nation does not deserve another three decades of dissension in the schools.

Notes

1. Complete information on average annual salaries of public school teachers from 1960 through 1996 in 1996 constant dollars is compiled by the National Center for Education Statistics ("The Condition of Education 1997, Supplemental Table 56–1"), available on the Internet at http//www.ed.gov/nces/index.html.

2. For a complete discussion of Deming's work applied to educational organizations and the barriers faced in America by proponents of the Deming approach, see *Teacher Unions and TQE,* by Streshly and DeMitchell, cited below. For a complete discussion of the Deming approach, see *Out of the Crisis,* by Deming, also cited below.

References

Brimlow, P., and L. Spencer. (1993). The National Extortion Association. *Forbes* 151(12), pp. 72–84.

Deming, W. E. (1986). *Out of the Crisis.* Cambridge: MIT Center for Advanced Engineering Study.

Lieberman, M. (1997). *The Teacher Unions.* New York: Free Press.

Streshly, W., and T. DeMitchell. (1994). *Teacher Unions and TQE.* Thousand Oaks, CA: Corwin Press.

Woo, E. (1996). "Blow Up the Schools: Albert Shanker's Last Stand." *New York Times Magazine* (December 1).

Appendix
Continuum of Employer–Employee Relationships

Relationship	Significant Characteristics
PATERNALISM	On the surface there is a good relationship between parties. The superintendent provides for all employee needs and regulates employee conduct. The relationship is based on the authority of the superintendent and is totally conditioned upon his or her goodwill. All the power rests with one person.
ENEMY	There is hostility toward the other party, a refusal to recognize its existence. The relationship is characterized by continuous challenges and threats to the other party.
ADVERSARY	There is a strong resistance to the other party, an arm's-length relationship with minimum acceptance and very strong defense, support, and maintenance of positions, proposals, and so on. Either party could accept destruction of the other but would not seek it. Some element of challenge to the other party still exists.
COLLABORATION	There is strong mutual acceptance of the other party, and the dominant approach is that of problem solving. The relationship is nonthreatening or nonchallenging. There is a willingness to submerge an advocacy relationship to gain broad objectives beneficial to both parties rather than just one.

MYTH 4:
SCHOOL BOARDS ARE GOOD FOR
AMERICAN EDUCATION

Introduction

Every school district in the United States is governed by a school board per state laws. School boards came into being more than 170 years ago, and they remain little changed from their inception. They continue to exist without demonstrating evidence that they are beneficial to the education of the children they are supposed to serve. Their success has been sparse. Why do they remain?

39

The American school board is a vestigial remain. We are familiar with vestigial remains in a biological sense as organs or appendages of a living body that at one time served a crucial role but now do not. They have survived beyond their purpose. Examples include the human tonsils, which at one time cleaned toxins from our body and fought infections. Another is the human appendix. This now idle remnant once served us nicely by aiding the body to digest food. Now, the appendix frequently causes life-threatening and debilitating illnesses. The good news is the swift surgical removal of these menacing vestigial remains. The bad news is that unlike the tonsil and the appendix that once served the body well, school boards have a long history of failure; there is also no swift or sure cure for the diseases they cause. In fact, there is strong reason to believe that as a disease, their effect is terminal. They have been immune to performance checks since their early-nineteenth-century sanctification in law.

◥

The Myth

Five school board members work late in the evening with the school district superintendent and the assistant superintendents. The agenda has been long, but a few important decisions are yet to be made in order to ensure high-quality educational opportunities for the community's young people. The board and superintendent are discussing a motion to place computers in the schools. The superintendent presented preliminary information at previous board meetings, sent informative documents to the board five days prior to this meeting, and called each member to answer their questions. The superintendent recommends the purchase of new computers, software, and training for the teachers and staff and presents the ten objectives of the purchase and an evaluation plan to assess the effects on student achievement.

To ensure a wise decision the board asks questions:

Will the use of computers be a new curriculum, or will they enhance the teaching of the existing curricula? Will all schools get computers?
What will be taught with the computers?
How much time will each child have on a computer?
Is the superintendent recommending a computer lab pullout program, or will the computers be placed in the classrooms?
How do the computers complement the curriculum? Do the school principals and teachers want the computers?
How do the computers fit into the district's long-range plan?
How will the success of the computer program be assessed and when?

When and what kind of information will be provided to the board to enable members to monitor progress and assess success?
Were funds allocated in this year's budget for this purchase?
Will any previously planned purchases be displaced?

The superintendent directs crisp and accurate answers to the questions. The board members deem the answers satisfactory and, with little adieu, approve a motion to follow through with the superintendent's recommendation.

That is the American school board in action, or is it? It is not. Instead it is an idealized scene Americans love to believe in. Those who perpetuate this myth of school boards love to believe that school boards efficiently and effectively focus on what students should learn, data-driven decision making, long-range goals, and the district's fiscal capabilities. This is a myth.

Promising Beginnings

Purveyors of this myth love to believe that, in a new country destined to be free of oppression by government, the school board represented the essence of local governmental control. The first school board was born in Massachusetts in 1826, when the legislature required each township to appoint a school board to oversee the schools. Today, school board members represent their community and safeguard it from state and federal control. With their power, school boards change curriculum, build facilities, and hire staff to meet the needs of the local youth and community. School boards have played a vital role in American education from the beginning. They set standards for learning excellence and moral development, based on local values. They ensure that these are delivered to students by establishing policies that direct the operation of schools.

Supporters of this myth argue that boards play a vital role in representative government, seeking consensus from the community and working with other board members to make major educational decisions regarding curriculum, school facilities, school taxes, class size, administrative staffing, and the like. Realizing that they are not trained educators, school boards hire professional staff to operate the schools in accordance with set policies. The boards empower their administration to run the schools in accordance with these decisions. Supporters of the myth claim that school boards have consistently limited their role to macromanagement. They devote themselves to the overall operation of the school district, that is, board members stay abreast of the district's progress through communiqués and close contact with the superintendent. They say that school board meetings provide the perfect venue for learning about school progress. Professional staff members provide data-driven reports to the board, and the board uses the data to make decisions about programs and directions. This process has worked wonderfully in keeping the district on track in pursuit of its mission—enhancing student achievement.

Supporters further claim that board members realize that they are not professional educators, so they eagerly seek training to help them fulfill this mission. They attend state and national training programs with their superintendent and continually work together to more effectively fill their role of oversight, or macromanagement. This role guides their service as board members. Daily affairs of the school such as placement of children in classrooms, student promotion and retention, selection of staff, and other day-to-day problems are left to the administration. Major responsibilities, such as establishing the district vision and long-range goals and monitoring district progress toward these goals, are macromanagement at its best. School board members realize that they have one vote on issues undertaken by the board. Realizing their macromanagement role, board members stay out of decision making in the day-to-day affairs of the schools.

Further, and unlike state and federal politicians, supporters of the myth claim that the school board member's purpose is undivided and altruistic. School board members do not use their elected positions for their own gain. They focus on student learning across the district and do not let personal interests or political gains mar the chaste and reverent purpose of their position as school board member. All decisions and actions are focused on bringing student learning to the highest levels possible.

Those who believe in this myth see schools boards as the last bastion of local representation. They continue to believe that these public servants are driven by the altruistic motive of ensuring that all children learn and that these servants work for free and ask for nothing in return.

The Reality

If this harmonious, objective, open, and efficient management style sounds familiar, you probably haven't been watching your local school board's behavior. Why? Because it is a myth. Narrow single views, personal biases, and petty politics all too often drive school boards. The goal is political gain and self-aggrandizement, not better education for students (see the cartoon). Any similarity between the efficient and effective scenario just described and most board meetings is accidental and unlikely. Here is a more likely scene.

"Why spend money on computers? Our high school state champion football team needs new uniforms to inspire the players and the fans.

After all, we have a tradition to maintain. People expect it. Mr. Superintendent?"

"What about word processing? These kids should learn to use a Windows format. We use Windows at work; it is the only way to go. Madam Superintendent?"

"Who cares about computers? What about this snow. Are you going to close school tomorrow, Mr. Superintendent?"

"Don't close school; my Ginger is scheduled to debate tomorrow and she will be heartbroken if it is canceled. She has been preparing diligently and this disappointment will devastate her! Well, Madam Superintendent?"

"Ah, come on, I gotta get up early. I move we table this computer stuff. Hell, I never had one and I am doing just fine, thank you! What a waste of money for a fancy typewriter! Well, Mr. Superintendent?"

"So what kind of computers are we going to buy? All I know is that with our local economy, the computers better come from our resident computer builder! Well, Madam Superintendent?" (This board member is also on the city board and is ready to announce plans to run for mayor.)

"Wow, it is snowing and the road looks dangerous. I second that motion and add that we meet again next week and direct the superintendent and his team to study this computer recommendation some more."

The meeting lasted four hours. Only the mundane decisions were made, all the curriculum and program decisions were tabled, and the administration was told to study more for the next meeting.

Sound unusual? Not by a long shot. Besides the superintendent, three other administrators were present at that meeting. Sixteen hours of administrators' time was wasted.

Humble and Regretful Beginnings

School board history is pockmarked with ineffectiveness and ineptitude. Lacking a clear role and appropriate training, the institution of school boards was flawed from the beginning, and failure was easily predictable.

Boards quickly realized that they needed a person to organize the board and run the schools. During their first one hundred years, boards frequently appointed the board secretary or other board member to be superintendent. "Indeed thirteen of Los Angeles's first twenty-three superintendents were laymen—doctors, lawyers, clergymen, and businessmen."[1] In San Francisco, the position was thrown into the political gristmill by giving the selection of superintendent over to popular elections. In other cities political cronies were appointed to the position by the mayor or city council. Still, in the 1930s the residents entered an election for office of superintendent. Slowly, professional educators replaced lay-people as superintendents.

The roles for the board and the superintendent have never been clear. From its inception the superintendency has been viewed with a jaundiced eye by laypeople's fear of "one-man control," the American bogey of long standing. Many teachers and principals did not want a superintendent for fear they would lose the autonomy they had in a totally decentralized system. Having unilateral control of the school(s), what were they going to do with a superintendent? What was this person going to do? Law did not assign duties, so superintendents garnered what authority they could from the board by winning its confidence. As we reveal, this has never been easy, and it has nearly always been political. Why a superintendent? Board members know the education process. They went to school and conducted education in their homes. All were experts. "The palladium of public liberty must be maintained" was their cry, and "no professional superintendents" was their exhortation! The concept of school boards represented an American ideal, one of local control and government by the people, a local training field in the politics of democracy and parlia-mentary procedure. It is a grand example of American spirit and home-spun American values and logic. Sounds good? You bet! The theory sounds good, but in practice the institution called the school board has been a failure. Boards have seldom served their community well, and they show little promise of improving. Not long after legislating their exis-tence and not being overly impressed with their actions, the Massachu-setts legislature began to corral the powers of local school boards. The legislature required the formation of a state board to control and system-atize the local school boards into a coherent system. The blame for the misdeeds and wrongdoings of the early boards should be shared by the Massachusetts legislature. After all, the legislatures, in their infinite wis-dom, started the process by legislating the creation of school boards and assigning them the duty to *oversee* their schools. With such a broad and vague job description the boards and the individual members struggled to determine their roles. Apparently not challenged by what would nor-mally be appropriate board duties, for example, determining what should be taught in school (the curriculum) and the length of the school day and year, the boards launched into matters of far greater interest.

Crucial Characteristics—Gender

One of the very first duties was the determination of gender eligibility for teaching. Must teachers be male or female? Or will either do? By divine revelation, or similar process, it was determined that females, only fe-males, would be those who form the immortal minds in home and school—that was the unique and vital role of women in a republic. Ms. Beecher gave this message to the trustees of the Hartford Female Seminary in 1829.[2] The idea was not hers alone. The revered Horace Mann, first secretary of the board for the state of Massachusetts, devoted his second annual lecture to the special qualifications of females. He spoke of "a divinely appointed ministry" in the "sacred temple of education."[3] Only women were fit for such an esteemed role. Such were the beliefs at the time. With the most important decision made, that of gender specification, school boards continued their search for a role and an identity (Bilken, 1995).

Teacher Duties

The duties of professional teaching had to be written. Following such officious images of "divinely appointed ministry" and "sacred temple of education," New York's Sullivan County[4] led the way in defining the work of the women fortunate enough to be elevated to teacherhood by writing the following truly important duties of teachers into their contracts:

- Sweep the floors at least once each day.
- Scrub the floor once each week with hot water and lye soap.
- Clean the blackboards daily.
- Start the fire at 7 A.M. so that the school room will be warm by 8 A.M.

What a slam to the citadel of strength and the grand position of teacher! What contradiction! What happened to the lofty duties befitting the title of "teacher"? To be sure, the board did not attempt to prescribe a teacher's entire day. In jest, we suggest that the early school boards set the stage for what we now know as decentralized, or site-based, decision making. Indeed, the selection of water temperature and day of the week to scrub floors was trusted to the teacher.

With these basic fundamentals of schooling determined, the boards garnered strength to tackle the truly tough issues of pedagogy— appearance and moral standards of the teachers. To this end the boards, relying on their astute insights and philosophies, cleverly and methodologically mandated that teachers will not

- dress in bright colors;
- wear the hem more than two inches above the ankles;
- wear more or less than two petticoats; and
- dry their petticoats where others can see them (dry them in pillow cases).

Well okay, bright colors and exposing the lower calf region of the leg are not hallmarks of a person holding a sacred job. But they were also not the hallmarks of sin and perdition. With this thinking, the board divined the following wise rules regarding teachers' personal deportment. Teachers shall not

- marry or keep in the company of men during their employment;
- get into a carriage or automobile with any man, except their brother or father;
- loiter at ice cream parlors;
- be out of the home between 8 P.M. and 6 A.M.;
- smoke cigarettes;
- dye their hair;
- miss a Sunday at church (and shall teach Sunday school and sing in the choir); or
- leave town without permission of the chairman of the school.

Sounds more like a code of conduct for prisoners. What about the critical elements of student learning: teaching and the curriculum? Did they not trust the women appointed to the divine ministry of teaching in the sacred temple of education? We find little solace in this provision.

Blind Leading the Blind: Legislatures and School Boards

The boards were quite pious, "holier than thou," in selecting their areas of interest, but who could blame them? The truth is that the legislature said school boards shall exist, but in regard to their duties, the law simply said the board shall "oversee" the operation of the school. With such vague direction, the boards were free to determine their chores, and they proceeded with haste to do just that. There are many well-documented examples of school boards and individual board members making fools of themselves, wasting administrators' time, and having negative influence on the students. Many of these poor, fumbling novices (and veterans) were well intended. They neither knew that their job was macromanagement nor knew how to do that job.

Ineptitude Revealed

Since their inception, school boards have dawdled and fussed over self-interests and political ideologies. Two independent reports prepared by private foundations and professional organizations in 1992 describe school boards, by in large, as failures.[5] Others say that school board governance is the biggest roadblock to substantive school reform. Others are even more vehement. They say that school boards have literally killed the institution called "school" (Lieberman, 1993).

In 1994 the Public Agenda Foundation and the Charles F. Kettering Foundation studied large and small school districts. They reported, "In each district, what started as a good faith effort to work together on school reform became a tug-of-war over turf." They observed widespread suspicion, anger, near-total distrust, and a lack of willingness to work together for the common good of their schoolchildren. As one superintendent noted, "Each special interest group is more concerned about the outcome for its particular group than for the common good."[6] Grand examples abound in every state. The Institute for Public Leadership (1992) found widespread problems from interviews, direct observations, and school board data. For example, boards

- are not providing far-reaching or politically risky leadership for educational reform;
- have become another level of administrations, often micromanaging the schools;
- are so splintered with special-interest groups that they cannot govern;
- do not educate themselves about policymaking (macromanagement);
- have not provided leadership with other agencies to meet student needs;
- do not have adequate policy oversight or accountability processes;
- do not act as impressively as their rhetoric in improving schools;
- have exhibited little capacity to develop positive and productive lasting relationships with their superintendents;
- do not evaluate their effectiveness; and
- in conflicted communities tend to make decisions in response to the issue of the day, while boards in more stable communities tend to govern to maintain the status quo (pp. 49–50).

The Report of the Twentieth Century Fund Task Force on School Governance (Danzberger, 1992) addressed many of these problems plus a few others. Boards

- lack the qualifications needed for school board service;
- lack an election system that holds them accountable for anything other than single interests; and
- lack adequate labor management skills.

Over our combined twenty-seven years as superintendents of schools, our experience with curriculum management audits, and our consulting work with school districts, we agree that these are problems. But this list is sterile in comparison to what the problems stand for in reality. A few colorful examples follow.

Board Members Know What's Best for All

In Vista, California, self-proclaimed fundamentalists and supposed saviors of society and their opponents dominated school board meetings with long, arduous speeches, threats of damnation, and reckless name-calling. So that's democracy at work in local government? Yes, but a terribly shoddy and destructive example. The students paid the price. No substantive improvements occurred in the school district during this turmoil, and thousands of work hours of educators' time that could have been used to improve education for young people were wasted. The fight goes on. In 1994, three school board members were up for recall. The superintendent said "enough of this" and won the superintendent's job in a not-too-distant school district. Teachers and administrators have exited. This nonexample of a smooth and productive democratic process more closely resembles the cooperation, patient listening, meaningful exchanges of ideas and ideals, and the *one-for-all and all-for-one* spirit of a pack of hyenas in a feeding frenzy. This public display of ineptitude and wrong-headed democracy in action is spreading across America.

Superintendent as Toy

In New York City, in 1993, a divided and bitter board of education chose Ramone C. Cortines, former superintendent in San Francisco, as their next chancellor, their sixth in ten years. The New York City School Board of Education has long been known for its political skulduggery; the fact that the past seven superintendents have been politically pulverized, rendered ineffective, and driven from the system by the board and their veiled political interests should have been a telltale sign to Mr. Cortines that he could be the next board toy.[7] But assuming the best, based on initial agreements to be a better board, he signed on the dotted line after a 4–3 vote. Unfortunately, the board did not change its vicious and meddling ways. Within months, fights erupted among board members, and political action groups and members conflicted with Mayor David Dinkins over his support of Mr. Cortines's chief rival for the job. This cleverly focused a laser beam on the fact that Mr. Cortines is Mexican-American. In reality, they saddled him with the job of disproving the suspicion that his selection had more to do with political rivalries and ethnicity than his merit as an educational leader.[8] This silliness serves no good purpose. The board is a laughing stock across the nation. Who could be proud of such nonsense? The answer is only those who think more highly of their deranged values than of the good of the children of New York City.

In this and many cases like it, the superintendent is a toy to the board—like the terrified field mouse appears to be a toy to a seemingly playful cat. The cat plays with the mouse, batting the little thing around until the mouse is played with to death. Superintendents have actually died from strokes and heart attacks on the job, and many have been rendered comatose. Many stay low and do nothing just to avoid the "play." Others seek and find greener pastures, only to find that they, too, turn brown. Others simply give up and await retirement.

Some board members believe that their superintendent is incompetent and assume that it is their responsibility to run the schools. Certainly some superintendents are incompetent; the authors could name a few, but that does not mean a board member should fill the slot! This scenario has taken many forms. During our curriculum management audit of the Large Stone School District, we have witnessed board members faxing multitudes of directives to school administrators. In one case we estimated that the directives of one board member, who faxed demands for reports directly to administrators, consumed hundreds of hours of administrators' time. In the district, a board member became very dismayed when his self-designed and self-ordered reports were not delivered on time and in a format to his liking. Such insubordination called for drastic action. Forthwith, the board member crashed the school offices to set the record straight. On more than a few occasions he boldly announced to all office staff and anyone else within hearing range that the administrator he was looking for "is a stupid son-of-a-bitch." Profound, indeed! Being quite colorful and not believing the superintendent to be a particularly attractive or good public speaker, he further shared his profundities (and his personal biases) by publicly directing the public relations department to keep that "skinny-lipped little witch off the air, she is a PR disaster." We wonder how he judged *himself* as a PR man?

In another major district, we estimated that just one (out of sixty-five) request for information consumed 6,800 hours of administrators' time.[9] What was the subject of the directives? Good question; undesirable answer. Most were to gather information the board member could use in his personal political battles, not official business of the district. Why? How many reports are needed? Is the information designed to improve schools? Only occasionally. The reports more frequently than not served to gain information slanted to support the board members' political agendas. They were not part of a district plan—just whims of individual board members who needed political fodder to fuel their launch to a higher political level. In doing so, they tarnished and degraded the palladium.

The Missing $1.9 Million, or, "We Have No Money for School Improvements"

During an audit of the Zeus School District, a real school district, the authors heard board members and administrators claim that funds did not exist to repair leaky roofs, to buy new and better materials for the students, or to train woefully incompetent teachers. But strangely enough, and after much digging and questioning, we learned that the eleven-member school board spends approximately $1.9 million dollars per year on their own and their staff's salaries. Now, what was that about lack of funds to make school improvements? What's wrong with this picture? Certainly something beneficial to schools could be accomplished with $1.9 million. Zeus School District is large with a big budget, but $1.9 million is not chicken feed. Funds for educational improvements were absolutely lacking. The board was forced to set priorities, and they chose to continue paying each board member $29,285 per year and to rehire one to three staff members for each board member. These staff members played the role of investigative reporters and quasi-administrators. They were not existing school administrators and secretaries. No, they were and are additional; their sole purpose is to staff the board members' fiefdoms. Surely $1.9 million was only a small portion of the budget. Leaking roofs and sufficient materials could wait, and they did. The effect? In fall 1997 the schools opened three weeks late. This was the third time in four years that the schools opened late because repairs were not completed. And what did the $1.9 million dollar purchase accomplish? Very little, other than financing election campaigns.[10]

School Boards Can Humble the Military's Best

In response to a longtime financially and educationally bankrupt school system, the federal government appointed a five-person financial-control board to govern the District of Columbia schools. One of their first moves was to ouster the superintendent. Not pleased with an educator as superintendent, they turned to the military for help and selected Julius W. Becton Jr. as superintendent. Mr. Becton previously served as director of the Federal Emergency Management Agency and as lieutenant general in the U.S. Army. Just sixteen months after his appointment as superintendent he declared that the superintendency has been his toughest job ever because of "so many competing interests" (Hendrie, 1998). Many of these could have been moderated or buffered by the federally appointed board. The politics of the public schools in Washington wore down and humbled even a tough military veteran. It is no wonder that superintendent turnover is so high, with the average length of service being less than three years. It is also no wonder that the superintendent's position is attracting fewer highly qualified candidates. Olson (1995) concludes that rapid turnover in leadership greatly impedes school improvement.

Highly esteemed research institutes and philanthropic foundations have declared that school boards are failures. They came blindly and unwittingly into existence, and they act with the demeanor of rabid dogs. Why do they exist? That is certainly a worthy question. The only reasonable explanation is inertia and weak-kneed politicians at the state level. Sundry publics, individuals, and foundations have cried for their elimination to no avail.

Other longtime successful democracies wonder why school boards exist in America. Japan tried the American school board plan and gave it up, finding fault with a system where the meddling of board members hinders the purpose of schools. "A strange artifact," they say.[11] If the American structure were superior, it would demonstrate greater performance, for example, in superior test scores, greater economic efficiency, and smoother labor relations. But it doesn't, and the evidence in fact favors structures used in some other countries. Another example is Germany, where the curriculum is set at a national level and the success of the schools casts a pall on the U.S. style of school governance.

What happened to the original altruistic motives for service on a school board? It is gone in many cities. Washington, Los Angeles, Boston, and Chicago school boards are just a few of those who pay their members. So, what do the schools get for the money? Is it a good purchase? What are the board members paid to do? Do they have a job description? Do they do the job well? Or do we even know? Has anyone set standards? If so, what are they? These are all legitimate questions. But 165-plus years of this costly and immoral high jinks have past. Does anyone care? What ever happened to the original idea that board members provide a service to the community? It is gone in many school districts. The palladium of public liberty is interpreted as a rightful possession to be milked for personal gain—not service responsibility to do good for our local communities. The rapacious need for self-serving power of many school board members is killing public education in America.

"Mr. Superintendent, you may not meet with the other board members!"—The Board President.

The San Diego newspapers have been full of funny but embarrassing stories regarding a local school board. Here is one: the subtitle reads "Grossmont trustee denounces LaChapelle move as 'palace coup.' " Mr. LaChapelle, then vice president of the board and one of three members of the board majority, issued a formal letter stating that the two nonmembers of the board majority were not to meet with the superintendent unless a member of the majority was present. What? Is Big Brother watching? we asked rhetorically. This directive slams the door on a prized First Amendment right, obliterates the superintendent's and individual board members' rights to meet and discuss school district business, and establishes the board majority as dominant dictators with full power to establish gag orders and shut down the democratic process. This outrageous yet silly behavior to cut communication between the superintendent and the two nonmembers of the board majority was moved farther away from the superintendent at the board meeting table by, of all things, placing the student board representative between them and the superintendent. This self-serving, nefarious move pulls the innocent student into the ugly political fray. But the student led the way. She simply said that she had no desire to be caught up in the conflict and did not care where she sat at the board table. Many observers hope that the board members learned a lesson in boardsmanship from the student, because the silly infighting among board members has taken a once highly successful school district and made it the laughingstock of education in Southern California—at student expense.

The Solution

As with the other solutions provided in this book, this one is not a secret. The Twentieth Century Fund Task Force on School Governance (Danzberger, 1992), the Institute for Public Leadership (1992), and numerous independent writers (Carver, 1997) have offered suggestions. We borrowed from many of these in developing the following recommendations.

First, state legislatures should rewrite all education statutes to clearly define and distinguish between macro- and micromanagement. Macromanagement should be assigned to school boards, and micromanagement should be assigned to the superintendent.

School boards should do the following:

- Hire a superintendent of schools.
- Scrutinize the proposed yearly budget to ensure it is in line with long-range planning and then adopt it.

- Establish policies for contracting and purchasing, and hire independent auditors to review the execution of these policies.
- Determine policies and guidelines for negotiating contracts with teacher organizations (when collective bargaining is authorized by state law).
- Establish a long-range plan, including short- and long-term goals with clear performance criteria, and stay with it. New goals may be added or goals may be deleted in accordance with the planning cycle.
- Approve curriculum, including goals and learning objectives for all students.
- Require staff development programs designed to improve student achievement through improved teaching and administrative practice and require stringent measures for assessing effectiveness.
- Serve as members of other community service boards to help link school efforts with those of private and public agencies to improve life for young people.
- Approve construction projects but, in policy, assign responsibility for approving change orders to the superintendent, who may do so for a community committee receiving assistance.
- Require the superintendent to provide data to demonstrate the district's progress in attaining district and school goals.
- Convene community forums on major policy issues to *hear* public opinion.
- Appoint groups comprising citizens and consultants to review key issues so that policy decisions are informed and explored before coming to the board.
- Focus at least 70 to 80 percent of board meeting agenda on reviewing curriculum programs, designing program directions and assessment requirements, reviewing assessment data, and modifying policy to ensure more effective learning. This is a formidable task, but it is doable and crucial. Considering that the product of schooling is learning, curriculum is the place to start. Board policies must be designed to guide district curriculum management.[12]

School boards should not:

- Exercise quasi-judicial responsibilities such as presiding over student or employee grievances; these should be assigned to the administration through policy.
- Require approval of small contracts and purchase orders that are bid

competitively, and small noncompetitive bids should be eliminated from board agendas.

- Require their approval of change orders within the limits set in policy.
- Hire, fire, or promote specific personnel, except for the superintendent and possibly deputy or associate superintendents. This means boards and individual board members will not interview prospective principals, directors, classified staff, and so on.
- Require approval of student field trips, inter- or intradistrict pupil transfers, specific staff development activities, and bus routes.

Sections of this chapter are a bit glib. Governing school districts is an infinitely important and highly difficult task. We think that board members must work to achieve the district's mission, yes, even if it means giving up individual interests and vendettas. School board positions are too often seen as stepping-stones to a political career, and that is a shame. The boards hold legislatively assigned responsibility and authority to run high-quality schools. The extensive information discussed in this chapter illustrates school boards' ineffectiveness. We do not say it is easy; successful reform will be difficult. We end with a message about the challenge to improve and those who gain from maintaining the status quo.[13]

> It must be remembered that there is nothing more difficult to plan, more doubtful of success, nor more dangerous to manage, than the creation of a new system. For the initiator has the enmity of all who would profit by the preservation of the institutions and merely lukewarm defenders in those who would gain by the new one.
>
> —Machiavelli

Notes

1. For a discussion of the process for awarding board positions, see Brubacher (1966, pp. 552–560).

2. To read the full transcript, see Beecher (1829), Suggestions Respecting Educational Improvement. Hartford, CT: Hartford Female Seminary.

3. For an interesting discussion of gender preferences for teachers, see Cremin (1980).

4. For a humorous yet accurate treatment of this subject see Feldman (1993).

5. These studies approach the subject of boardsmanship from different perspectives but arrive at the same conclusion. See the Institute for Public Leadership (1992) and Danzberger (1992). For an excellent historical review of the American

school board in action over the past hundred years, see "Who's in Charge," *Education Week*, vol. 19, no. 12, p. 1.

6. For further discussion, see (no author) *New York Times*, vol. 142, no. 49,292, section A p. 14.

7. Superintendent Rudy Crew had made major strides in the New York City schools and was recently run out of office during a political run-in with Mayor Rudolph Guiliani. On January 19, 2000, the New York City School Board hired Harold O. Levy, the school interim chancellor ("Giving Mr. Levy a Chance," *New York Times*, vol. 149, no. 51,273, p. 22). The editorial announced that the appointment was as least mercifully free of the acrimony that dominated the last ten days, when Mayor Rudolph Guiliani said he would seek court action to prevent the appointment.

8. See (no author) *New York Times*, vol. 142, no. 49,440, section A p. 10.

9. This finding comes from a real school district. Legal requirements prevent the authors from revealing the actual name of the district.

10. To the board's credit, they did forgo a raise in 1995.

11. For a thorough discussion of the Japanese opinion, see Takeaki Nakadome (1993).

12. For elaboration on each policy area and the entire curriculum management audit, see chapter 5 in Frase, English, and Poston (1994).

13. This chapter unveils the quirks and warts of many school boards and school board members, but this chapter should not be interpreted as saying that all board members and all boards of education are ineffective or diabolical. We have worked with and associated with many fine school board members. We do not wish to offend these people; they did their job very well. We think you know who you are. We have also worked with a few nut cases, and we have no compunction for them. If they feel offended, they should—they are the warts.

References

A Curriculum Audit of the Little Rock School District. (1990). Arlington, VA: American Association of School Administrators.

A Curriculum Audit of the Zeus School District Public School. (1992). Arlington, VA: American Association of School Administrators.

Bilken, S. (1995). *Gender and the Cultural Construction of Teaching*. New York: Teachers College, Columbia University.

Brubacher, J. (1966). *A History of the Problems of Education*. New York: McGraw-Hill.

Carver, J. (1997). *Boards That Make a Difference: A New Design for Leadership in Nonprofit and Public Organizations*. San Francisco: Jossey-Bass Publishers.

Cremin L. (1980). *American Education: The National Experience, 1973–1876*. New York: Harper and Row.

Danzberger, J. (1992). *Facing the Challenge: School Governance*. New York: Twentieth Century Press.

Feldman, B. (1984). "Great Expectations of Yesteryear's Teacher." *New York Times*, May 6, p. 22E

Frase, F., F. W. English, and W. K. Poston. (1994). *The Curriculum Management Audit: Improving School Quality*. Lancaster, PA: Technomic Publishing Company.

Hendrie, C. (1998). "D.C. Schools Chief Announces Resignation." *Education Week* 17:29 (April 1).

Institute for Public Leadership. (1992). *Governing Public Schools: New Times New Requirements*. Zeus School District: Institute for Public Leadership.

Lieberman, L. (1993). *Public Education: An Autopsy*. Cambridge: Harvard University Press.

Nakadome, T. (1993). "Three Views from Abroad: A Japanese Perspective." *American School Board Journal* 8:50, pp. 8–12.

Olson, L. (1995). "Rapid Turnover in Leadership Impedes Reforms." *Education Week* 14:16, p. 6.

MYTH 5:
SELF-ESTEEM MUST COME FIRST—
THEN LEARNING

Introduction

Wherever we've turned these past thirty years we found book after book and program after program espousing the virtues of high self-esteem, and the need for public schools to teach it. Education lectures are packed with it. It seems to be a mantra of the National Education Association (NEA). Parent organizations wildly seek ways to help children feel good about themselves. When interviewing teachers and administrators, we frequently hear that high student self-esteem is the number-one goal and must precede all else. We challenge this notion.

The Myth

The myth is that students must feel good about themselves before they can learn. Supporters of this myth defend it with religious fervor. This conviction is not without reason. No one we know defines a successful life as one where the person feels lousy about him or herself. Feeling good is nice; it is the way we want to feel. But to think that students must feel good about themselves before they can learn is silly, myopic thinking. We have never observed a student or adult who felt good about being illiterate or ignorant. Sound funny? Only in a perverted sense, as illustrated by Billy's friend in the cartoon.

The following are just a few examples of the faddish silliness people have about self-esteem:

- A Native American teacher in a southern Arizona school district we audited shared her wisdom with us: "You know, these children [i.e., Native American] can't learn much. My job is just to love them."
- In schools across our nation, fifth- and sixth-grade girls are asked to make a list of eight qualities they like about themselves. Each good quality is written on a paper petal to form a flower, then a photo of each girl is placed in the center of her own flower. Teachers, parents, and administrators in these school districts say this activity is necessary since self-esteem is requisite to learning the basics, even though the activity is divorced from a larger lesson and cognitive gains.
- Educators in Large City School District, Texas; Inglewood, California; Washington, D.C.; and many other cities with high concentrations of African American and Hispanic teachers told us that "these poor kids are so oppressed they are not ready to learn; our first job is to show them love and help them feel good about themselves."
- Critics of today's bilingual education programs say that the underlying belief that Hispanic students must develop their self-esteem before they can learn is silly, whereas bilingual education proponents say doing otherwise is unwise and potentially debilitating.
- The feel-good efforts in California have failed. Companies spend huge sums of money to teach the state's high school graduates sim-

ple basic skills. Meanwhile, California universities are providing remedial mathematics and English to thousands of students, all of whom graduated in the top third of their high school classes. The education system believed that self-confidence and high self-esteem are the best ways to enhance confidence, and that this would improve scholastic achievement and good citizenship in general.

- The self-esteem myth was summarized by one of our graduate students, a teacher in administrative training: "If a child comes to school without getting a good night's sleep, it is okay if he sleeps in class. He feels better when he wakes up. After all, the child has problems at home that render the three Rs less important."

The Reality

Feeling good about yourself is a wonderful *by-product* of learning, not the *cause* of it. It happens naturally and without external inducement. It happens when we achieve, when we do something well.

The wonderful news is that many students want stronger teaching and standards. The beleaguered and low-achieving Chicago schools are adopting higher standards. New York is in the process of beefing up its standards by requiring all high school students to pass a battery of college-preparatory Regents tests rather than the much less stringent Regents Competence Test (RCT). Many students want tougher tests. New York City students' reactions to tougher tests have been positive. A freshman recently said, "We are the class of 2000; at least we know that when we graduate, we deserve to graduate." Another said, "This [the Regents test] is a better test. The RCT feels like you're back in kindergarten." In a national study, students told the Public Agenda Organization (1997) that higher standards are not enough; they want "more attentive, demanding teachers." Further, they say that they

- admire students who do well in school;
- want more of a challenge to get their diploma ("we can glide; grades are given to us");
- believe there are too many disruptive students in class, that discipline is lax or nonexistent;
- want, like most adults desire, to be taught how to work hard;
- want better teachers, and more attention from teachers would help them achieve higher standards (63 percent said this); 23 percent think that this would help them most;

- want interesting, engaging teachers who have a special knack for getting them to do their best;
- respect the demands and consistency from drill sergeant–type teachers; and
- want students to be more respectful of teachers.

Parents, too, want their children to learn. A Los Angeles–based reporter for the *New York Times* recently told of a Mexican national couple who came to Los Angeles with their family to work in sweatshops so that their children could learn English and receive a fine education. After finding that the schools would not teach their children English, they refused to allow their children to attend school. They wanted their children to learn English (Callaghan, 1997). They were not alone. Seventy other poor immigrant families joined them in February 1996, insisting that their children be allowed out of the bilingual program and that they be taught English in English. These and many more Latino parents backed a California ballot initiative designed to end bilingual education for most children in the state. They feared that bilingual education programs were keeping their children from learning English in favor of maintaining and establishing their self-esteem. After twenty-five years, bilingual education has very few defenders among Latino parents. In a recent *Los Angeles Times* poll, 83 percent of Latino parents in Orange County said they wanted their children to be taught in English as soon as they started school. These parents know that unless their children become literate in English, their poverty cycle will not end. Only 17 percent said they favored having their children taught in their native language.

The reality is that the dropout rate for Hispanics aged sixteen to twenty-four is 30 percent, nearly double that of whites and blacks. A recent study in New York City showed that 90 percent of the students who started bilingual education in the sixth grade were unable to pass an English-language test after three years of bilingual instruction. Yet English as a second language and non-English-speaking students are required to enroll in bilingual programs. The folly here is that a law was recently passed that requires immigrants from Caribbean nations who speak or understand a Creole language and score in the bottom 40 percent on an English-language test to be instructed in bilingual education. Had these children stayed in their Caribbean home, they would have been instructed in English.[1]

Totally contrary to the self-esteem enthusiasts, higher percentages of African American students, educators, and parents believe that academics are "extremely important" in finding a job than do non–African American students. Black and white parents are very adamant about the importance of academic achievement to their children. When asked what the priority for schools should be, 80 percent of black parents and 66 percent of white parents chose raising academic standards and achievement over integration (Farkas and Johnson, 1998). We maintain that after twenty-five years of research there is virtually no substantive evidence that high self-esteem must come first before academic learning can occur. We believe that teachers, and for that matter all adults, should respect student psyches, but self-esteem is not requisite to learning. Contrarily, learning enhances self-esteem. Purveyors of this myth actually agree, albeit unwittingly (Maeroff, 1998),[2] when they conclude that learning and overcoming challenges result in higher self-esteem.

In fact, the highly touted $735,000 California Task Force on self-esteem came to the conclusion that the relationship between self-esteem and learning is weak. Hold on to your seat: a common finding is that high self-esteem is often linked to low performance. The deeply seated belief that America's history of racial oppression resulted in low self-esteem for African Americans is also false. African American self-esteem is as high as and sometimes higher that that of whites (Rothman, 1989). The author tells us that we live in a time of irrationality; widely refuted but firmly seated beliefs continue. For example, the idea that violence is committed by people of low self-esteem is essentially false. In fact, people committing violence tend to have higher self-esteem than those who do not. Roy Baumeister's (1996) research shows that violence is more commonly committed by people with unrealistically high self-esteem. He warned that certain forms of high self-esteem are correlated to narcissism and seem to increase violence, and that unabated efforts to enhance self-esteem may be counterproductive, dangerous, and may literally end up doing considerable harm. The reality is that people develop legitimate self-esteem when they achieve something good and worthwhile, not until then.

Harold Stevenson (1992) studied education in Asia and in the United States for ten years. One of his many research findings is that although Asian students performed far better than American students, American students felt much greater satisfaction about their school achievement. He also found that 70 percent of the Chinese students said education was very important. Only 10 percent of American students mentioned education; they valued money and things. Similarly, Asian parents said that the most important thing for their kids is to work hard and do well in school. American parents said doing well in school is just one among a number of things—kids should be popular and good in sports.

The trend is clear—and not related to "self-esteem." American parents and students also lack faith in the efficacy of hard work in school. Asian parents believed that their students needed to work hard through the twelfth grade before they could predict achievement on college entrance tests. American parents said that the prediction could be made in the sixth grade. In other words, Americans believed that ability, not work, was what counted. They hold schooling in "low" esteem. When asked the most important factor in math performance, 70 percent of the Japanese and 60 percent of the Taiwanese students said "studying hard." Only a little more than 20 percent of American students mentioned work, and 55 percent attributed success to having a good teacher. If they did not do well in school, it was due to poor schools or poor teaching.

A study by Nathan Caplan (1992) supports Stevenson and offers powerful evidence to support the efficacy of hard work. He found that poor Indo-Chinese refugee students with little or no English-language skills, who had lost months and years of schooling during their escape from Asia and their time in relocation camps, went to schools in poor, inner-city areas. Nevertheless, 27 percent achieved an *A* average and more than 50 percent a *B* average. Half of them scored in the top 25 percent in mathematics. These families clear the table after dinner, and the students do their homework and help each other. They exert effort.

The reality is that all industrialized countries scoring higher than the United States hold students accountable for their learning. Self-esteem is not the issue.

These findings and common sense tell us that the "can do," work hard ethic is missing in too many schools and families. We suggest achievement is what fosters high self-esteem. For example, name the two events that occurred to you in high school that you felt best about. The vast majority of people name an achievement, accomplishing something. Few, if any, name a touchy-feely activity. We bet the teachers involved in your event enforced standards, wanted you to do well, told you to do well, and acted as though they cared more about your learning than your self-esteem. Ours did.

The Solution

The solution is obvious. Focus schools on the product: learning. Happy kids and high self-esteem are natural—they result from achieving. Here are the key ingredients:

- Announce that the product of one's school district is learning, and then run the schools to achieve that end.
- Focus schools, administrators, and teachers on ensuring that only high-quality instruction occurs in the schools.
- Focus schools on doing what they can to provide highly effective

learning environments, and rid the pathways to learning of road-blocks.

- Teach parents and educators that hard work is good and necessary, that struggle is not a bad word, and that good things come with effort.
- Teach parents that they have the primary responsibility to require their children to do homework and hold *them* accountable for their success and failures.
- Teach parents, educators, and students that high self-esteem is the result of achievement, not the cause of it—that doing a worthwhile task or job well results in good feelings.

The solution is for schools to disabuse themselves and their communities of the myth that self-esteem must come first. Next, they must accept the empirically and scientifically proven wisdom that hard work leads to achievement and feeling good is a wonderful natural by-product.

Notes

1. For an interesting discussion see D. Ravitich (1997), "First Teach Them English," *New York Times*, vol. 146, no. 50,906, section A, p. 21.

2. For a review of unwitting agreement with our position and the folly of proposed myth, see Maerhoff (1998) wherein he claims, and rightly so, that students with low self-regard may resist learning. He then proceeds to tell stories about how learning how to do something (e.g., kayaking, rope climbing, and so on) results in higher self-regard and confidence.

References

Baumeister, R. (1996). "Relation of Threatened Egotism to Violence and Aggression." *Psychological Review* 103(1): 5–33.

Callaghan, A. (1997). "Desperate to Learn English." *New York Times*, August 15, p. A15.

Caplan, N., M. Choy, and J. Whitmore. (1992). "Indochinese Refugee Families and Academic Achievement." *Scientific American* 266(2) (February): 37–42.

Farkas, S., and J. Johnson. (1998). *Time to Move On: African-American and White Parents Set an Agenda for Public Schools.* New York: Public Agenda Foundation.

Maeroff, G. I. (1998). "Altered destinies: Making life better for schoolchildren in need." *Phi Delta Kappan* 79:424–432.

Rothman, S. (1989). *The Myth of Black Low Self-Esteem.* Northampton, MA: Smith College Center for the Study of Social and Political Change.

Stevenson, H. (1992). *The Learning Gap.* New York: Summit Books.

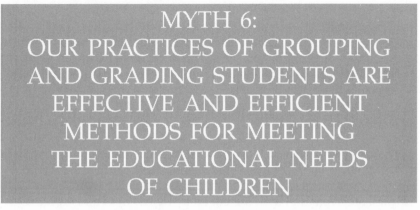

MYTH 6:
OUR PRACTICES OF GROUPING AND GRADING STUDENTS ARE EFFECTIVE AND EFFICIENT METHODS FOR MEETING THE EDUCATIONAL NEEDS OF CHILDREN

Introduction

"An *F* to the school board . . . and to public schools too!" That was the headline on the editorial page of the local newspaper after the San Diego Board of Education announced that teachers will be prohibited from dispensing *F*s. Instead, students who fail classes would receive a "no credit," which would not count against their grade point average. To make matters worse, the newspaper reported, the elementary students who in the past would have been held back a grade would now be promoted automatically. After railing about everything from the inevitable "watering down" of academic standards to America's growing competitive disadvantage in the global marketplace (San Diego was experiencing a minor recession at the time), the editorial concluded by pronouncing, "Failure is a fact of life. The sooner San Diego students are fully apprised of that fact, the better prepared they will be to avoid its unpleasant consequences."

The great significance of this editorial is not the criticism against a school board's action. Rather, it is significant because it represents the man on the street's idea about what makes schools good. Thousands of San Diegans applauded as the editor pontificated, "Failure and fear of failure are great motivators in school—and in life long after graduation."

The Myth

The San Diego editor and millions of Americans ardently embrace a paradigm for public education that was invented in America during the dawning of the industrial age and has remained unchanged since. The paradigm decrees that students about the same age be gathered together in classes, or "grades." It assumes that since the children are all about the same age, they are all at about the same stage of development and have about the same needs. This means the states and school districts can develop appropriate, "standard" curricula for each of these grade levels and can test the students from time to time to see whether they are learning at the official rate. The belief undergirding this Procrustean practice is that all students can be successful if they pay attention, work hard, and diligently do what the teacher requires. In this setting, failure is seen as "real life" and students will benefit from its lessons. The ones who try but still fail are judged to be defective in some way and therefore are certified for "special" education.

The paradigm is also based in the belief that tests are a reflection of student progress, in other words, whether they are paying attention, working hard, and diligently meeting the teacher's requirements. In this system, so the story goes, if teachers taught as well as they could teach and students worked as hard as they could work, everyone would succeed. Naturally, the difficulty of the curriculum content specified for each grade level makes a difference. A decade or so ago, school leaders in Dallas tried to stem the rising failure rate in their district by cutting back on the amount of classroom material that had to be covered each school year.

It didn't work. Some students continued to fail while others were bored stiff. Sound familiar?

The solution to problems like this traditionally has been to tinker with the system by creating "gifted" or "honors" classes for the top students and "learning disabled" or "behavior disorder" or "resource specialist" classes for the bottom students. This doesn't work either, and it turns out to be horribly expensive. Tinkering with the organization doesn't work because it does not attack the fundamental problem.

The Reality

Our school programs are built around the practice of grading and rating, sifting and sorting. It may sound cruel to say, but we really don't expect or want all students to succeed. Even though thousands of school districts include the old saw "all students can succeed" as a part of their mission statements, they don't believe it. The real belief system is rock-solid, and it pervades all educational institutions from kindergarten through graduate school. It goes something like this: some students are naturally brighter than others, and our task is to sort them out and put them in programs where they can succeed. To make sure the system accomplishes this sorting task, administrators from kindergarten through high school review the student grade distributions of their various faculty members. A teacher who gives all *A*s is subject to as much scrutiny as the one who gives all *F*s. The message is clear. If you are giving all *A*s, you are not upholding the "standards" of the institution.

A large number of low grades is not acceptable either, because of the political pressure from angry parents and students. Most teachers trim to a middle course and develop their programs in a way that will produce a more or less "normal" distribution of grades. Still, it is not uncommon to hear teachers at the secondary level actually boast of the number of *F*s awarded to their students. The implication is that they are upholding the standards for their departments.

As beginning teachers we were curious about this phenomenon. We wondered why some teachers would brag about failures. In contrast, the football coach didn't brag at all about his losses, but then again the football coach and his staff were doing everything in their power to make certain the students succeeded—even if it meant making hundreds of modifications to their system to accommodate individual strengths and weaknesses.

We soon learned that the difference was in the mission. The coach's mission was to produce a team that performed well, not to rank and rate each player. Yes, judgments are made by the coach continuously to diagnose weaknesses and correct them, but the objectives of the coach and the student are to teach well and perform well, not to give a grade and get a grade. When the San Diego editor remarked, "Hardly anyone values something that is attained with little or no effort," he was indisputably talking about grades, not knowledge. Profound knowledge and skill would be valued even if it were attained with little or no effort. He was referring to a grade that was attained with little effort. We say, "So what?"

The practice of "grading tough" is an undeniable symbol for academic standards. First-grade teachers retain their slow starters because they don't want the second-grade teachers to think they are not upholding the standard or teaching the students the curriculum. And they do this in spite of their awareness of the overwhelming body of research proclaiming that retention does not help children to catch up.[1] In fact, it puts them at much greater risk for future failure than their equally achieving, nonretained peers. The paradigm of sifting and sorting students has created a compelling cultural ethic demanding conformity throughout the system.

To make matters worse, schools of teacher education prepare teachers and administrators for this paradigm of schooling. Textbook publishers design materials and texts based on this model. In other words, the prospects of changing the public schools behemoth are daunting, to say the least. To avoid head-on confrontations, knowledgeable school leaders dodge public condemnation by surreptitiously modifying programs in order to better serve children. In other words, they sidestep the problem. In Texas, for example, the legislature ordered that no student who failed the eighth grade could pass on to high school—all in the name of higher standards and greater accountability. Very soon there appeared "schools within schools" at various high schools. On closer examination, it turns out that these schools within schools are "junior high schools" on the high school campuses—a loophole allowing failing junior high students to pass on to the high schools. In most cases, the students take their eighth-grade core subjects together in a homogeneously grouped "junior high school" class and their electives (physical education, shop, band) with the general student body. We are sure that this is not what the legislature had in mind, but it is certainly a lesser evil.

Several schools across the nation have experimented with giving no grades in primary classes (grades K, 1, 2, 3). These programs usually get off to a good start because students are allowed to grow at their own paces and are generally happier about school. Naturally, some of the students don't do as well as others, and parents turn to the school for more information about how their students compare with other students. Invariably, they want to know their *grades*. Over and over, school districts that use nonstandard grading systems designed to give parents maximum information about their children without assigning nominative grades run into this snag. Whatever the system, parents demand to know what the equivalent *A* to *F* grade would be—if their students were being graded. The time of reckoning comes, of course, when the students move from this more nurturing environment to a class with standard grades and more traditional curricula. Some students receive poor grades, and parents then criticize the school for "keeping them in the dark."

In light of the profound impact that grades have had on our public school system, it is interesting to note that grading and grouping are fairly recent advents, dating back no earlier than the mid-nineteenth century.[2] They emerged as a response to government support of elementary schools and high schools that exploded the number of students. The number of public high schools increased from about five hundred in 1870 to more than ten thousand in 1910. School districts were forced to consider ways of organizing classes more efficiently. They began to use percentage scales to help them differentiate among students of various academic aptitudes. One thing led to another. Age groupings led to groupings by percentile grades, producing homogeneous groups with the intent of making mass education more efficient. More high school graduates meant greater competition for admission to colleges. Scores or grades became a great help in screening applicants. Around this same time, colleges began to use grading systems (Milton, Pollio, and Eisen, 1986). Yale was the first, awarding four grades: *optime, second optime, inferiors,* and *perjores.*

This new practice of awarding grades created a curious change in the American view toward teaching and learning. Under the old system, if the students didn't make satisfactory progress, the teachers were criticized. Perhaps their jobs were in jeopardy. With grades, accountability was shifted away from the teachers to the students (Hargis, 1990). The news in 1997 that the Chicago School Board would fire teachers whose students failed represents a move back to the future. As soon as the news hit the mass media, other school boards around the country applauded.

Grading Is the Problem

The truth of the matter is that our system of sifting and sorting students stands clearly in the way of any meaningful reform in this country. The American people feel that grades are motivating, but the fact is that for the large bulk of students, they are discouraging. Only the top students are stimulated by their good grades. Failing students who are moved to one of the myriad special education programs or who are assigned one of the plethora of special services usually continue to fail. Very plainly, there is no evidence to suggest that a poor grade will stimulate a failing student to do better work. Moreover, grades don't provide worthwhile targets or goals for most students. More than likely, high grades are unattainable for the poor students, and the best students are far beyond the standard curriculum.

School administrators often justify evaluation and grades on the basis that parents need the information. In reality, grades tell parents very little about how much or what a student has learned. Usually they only show how well the student is doing compared to other students in his classroom based on the tests completed, homework handed in, and other criteria established by the teacher. In order to interpret grades, parents also need to know the neighborhoods served by the school and the socioeconomic status of the student population. An *A* in a wealthy suburban school is definitely not equivalent to an *A* in an inner-city school. Grades also differ widely from teacher to teacher. Many teachers have been influenced with the studies on damage done to students by grades and have begun to give higher marks, contributing to monumental grade inflation over the last thirty years. In 1967, straight-*A* graduates were rare. By 1997, most high schools had a dozen or more each year. In June 1998, one Southern California high school boasted forty-two straight-*A* valedictorians. With the advent of weighted grades, all students in the top 10 percent of some high schools have grade averages above 4.0.

This is not a criticism of the many dedicated professionals in the field. Rather, it is a condemnation of the old, industrial age model within which they are struggling. Ironically, most children can succeed to some extent in our current system and make reasonable academic progress. Unfortunately, this fact helps perpetuate the system—a system in which fully 25 percent of our students do not fit and in which they cannot succeed.

Passing the Buck, Not the Students

The behavioristic practice of assigning grades to students hinders their progress in most cases. Most of our teachers are aware of the destructive potential of grades, and they recognize the signs of frustration and alienation that began to develop within the students at grades 3 and 4 and that become prominent by the end of middle school. Oddly, no one wants to point the finger at the grading system. Teachers blame lazy students, drugs, and bad parents. There is nothing new about this.

More commonly these days (and more tragically), teachers are blaming so-called handicaps. If the student can't read, teachers blame it on a handicapping condition called dyslexia. On closer examination, however, we find that dyslexia simply means, "Can't read." More circular finger-pointing results in unruly students being labeled with a "behavior disorder" and slower students being labeled as "learning handicapped." This sad state of affairs would be humorous if it weren't tragic. One school district in Illinois spends more than 30 percent of its instructional budget on special education and serves 18 percent of its student body with expensive special programs. What's more, the percentage of special education is still growing in this struggling district, and as the regular education classes get larger, more "handicapped" students are produced. The result is a downward spiral of overall student performance accompanied by an upward spiral of costs.

Many of our nation's most successful citizens have had difficulty in school and dropped out. They succeeded—in spite of their schooling. We don't need to spend time listing the names. Most of you are familiar with them, and most of them were described as "late bloomers." In other words, they developed slowly. The fact that they succeeded in spite of our schools is often a credit to their families or some other fortunate encounter. But we can't escape the bitter fact that we have developed a school system in our country that tends to weed out these late-blooming geniuses, and the culprit is our system of grading and grouping.

The Argument for Change

Changing our public schools' grading and grouping paradigm will require nothing less than a cultural transformation. Schools are a part of our political system, and they don't change based on rational data—unless nobody cares. When the American Association of Health, Physical Education, and Recreation recommended that trampolines be removed from high schools because they were too dangerous, the trampolines were removed. The pressure group behind trampoline use in high schools was virtually nonexistent. Consequently, a good decision was "allowed" to happen. A few years later, when varsity football was estimated to be one hundred times more dangerous than trampolines, the public school response was to buy more liability insurance.

Horror stories abound concerning the fallout from grading practices. For example, in a society that would like to be a moral leader in the world, cheating in our schools is at an all-time high—from kindergarten through graduate school, from medical schools to military academies. Among very young children it is a matter of the lesser of two evils: committing an academic transgression or displeasing parents. In the lower grades, students often can't distinguish between *bad,* meaning *immoral,* and *bad* meaning *failure to achieve in the top half of the class.* In desperate attempts to avoid being "bad" in the eyes of their parents, thousands of these children each year learn to cheat.

Other students frustrated with failing find themselves daydreaming about better times and more pleasing surroundings. Since dropping out is usually not an option for eight-year-olds, these students suffer quietly in class, falling farther and farther behind. Eventually, these daydreamers are labeled with attention deficit disorder or some other contrived malady and are weeded out of the regular classes. Usually the only symptom these students display is failure to keep up with the norm. In many cases this may be a temporary condition caused by some upset in the family, or an inability to fully understand the teacher, or, like Einstein, he simply learns slowly (and it is proper to use the pronoun *he* in this case since nearly nine out of every ten so-called learning-handicapped students are boys). Tragically, most of these "labeled" students never fully recover. As one Illinois administrator lamented, "Their [special education] sentence is usually a life sentence." They continue to lag behind their classmates and their peers for the remainder of their schooling, and in the absence of a significant intervention, they will lag behind their peers for the rest of their lives.

One such student with whom we're acquainted followed the typical pattern. Labeled "slow" in elementary school, he lagged farther and farther behind, and soon even the allure of high school athletics couldn't keep him coming to school. He dropped out and went to work for a local agricultural pump company. Cranky, as he was known, was a popular boy—affable, self-confident in social situations, and possessing a good sense of humor. Eventually, he married his high school sweetheart and settled down in his hometown, where he and his wife made a meager living at low-level wages. Then one day—twelve years after he dropped out of high school—Cranky made a life-changing decision. In his words, "I was tired of earning a minimum wage to explain to the engineers why the pumps wouldn't work. When they finally understood, they would agree with me and instruct me to fix it in the manner I had suggested it be fixed. Only they were making the big bucks. So I talked it over with the wife, and I went back to [a local community college]."

Cranky was lucky. He had a smart, supportive wife, and soon he learned that the labels he had carried since elementary school were wrong. He began earning the top grades in his class, especially in math. He went on to the University of California–Berkeley for his degree in civil engineering. By this time his academic record made him good enough to be picked up by one of the world's largest construction companies, where he eventually wound up in charge of engineering groups building atomic reactors. Unfortunately, most victims of our grading and sorting procedures are not as lucky.

Students sorted into the upper groups are not necessarily winners in the system either. Many gifted classes pile on mind-numbing workloads. Often students put into gifted classes during their elementary school years are awarded blanket A's in recognition of their status as gifted students. These children get the idea that almost anything they do is of high quality. The system's obsession with assigning a normative grade ranking the work of these students with all other students causes them to overlook some of the fundamentals. As one freshman high school English teacher put it, "The big difference between my college prep class and my gifted class is the gifted students can't organize their ideas or punctuate their sentences." Years of elementary school gifted classes had allowed these youngsters to explore their creative impulses without engendering in them the craft discipline of writing. At one high school, this was known by the teachers as "the Pop Warner [youth football] syndrome." All-American Pop Warner football players at age twelve were often surprised to find that they were unable to maintain their All-America status when they began playing high school football without weight-class restrictions. The difference between 145-pound Pop Warner players and 245-pound high school players often presented more frustration than these early achievers could handle. So they quit trying and dropped out. Labeling eight-year-olds "gifted" is dangerous for similar reasons. The practice, needless to say, is very popular with the parents of these children. The gifted label, as illustrated in the cartoon, allows the proud parent *bragging rights*.

But it is not the early achievers who suffer most. Young students who are given failing grades suffer trauma, and repeated failure will have an unmistakable impact that the child may never overcome. In spite of overwhelming research, this idea continues to be pooh-poohed by the general public, politicians, advocates of the school of hard knocks, and even educational politicians. "We've got to prepare our kids for a rough-and-tumble competitive life." The rough-and-tumble schooling that the American public supports flunks more than *two million elementary-aged students per year* (i.e., they are not allowed to pass on from one grade to another). These students will be five times more likely to drop out when they reach high school (Shepard and Smith, 1990). Even when other factors are controlled for, such as the level of parental education, retained students are 20 to 30 percent more likely to drop out of school. Studies of retained students in the early grades reveal that fear of not passing onto the next grade was equal to wetting one's pants in class. In another study, children listed only two life events as more stressful than being retained: going blind and losing a parent.

Probably the final insult is the enormous financial cost we pay for our grading and grouping practices. Despite the fact that sorting students by age, by achievement, and by handicap was originally set up to be more efficient, it has turned out to be vastly more expensive. The cost of requiring two million children to repeat a grade each year alone is a whopping $10 billion—even after adjusting for the higher dropout rate of these students. And this figure does not include other, less direct effects, such as low productivity or the antisocial tendencies of dropouts.

The Solution

So if the American-grown tradition of grading and sorting is a proven failure, why don't we do something about it? First and foremost, the American public clings desperately to a sacrosanct belief in the efficacy of grading students and upholding standards by failing some of them. As former public school administrators, we must confess to succumbing to the unrelenting political pressure. We have supported policies that set rigid, lockstep, grade-by-grade curriculum standards and grading practices and that call for students to repeat a grade if they do not measure up to predetermined levels of achievement. We were fully aware that these policies sacrificed the best interests of individual children to appease popular public demands and to assure a good showing on the state's tests. But by no means are we alone. Educators in every state are guilty. In Georgia, even kindergartners can flunk and be turned away from first grade.

Turning the tide of public opinion in America, especially on a topic as bitterly debated as this one, is an intimidating task. We mentioned previously that teachers are locked into a "standard" curriculum at every grade level. Students who aren't taught the standard curriculum will not test well on the standard tests administered by the state (see Chapter 2, on national testing). Low test scores mean embarrassed administrators, state sanctions, and so forth. Needless to say, teachers will be strenuously encouraged to teach the standard curriculum to all students in the class as long as the statewide accountability tests are in the political picture. This guarantees frustration and failure for some students who are not ready to learn the material. It also means boredom for other students who wait for the slow ones to catch up. "And that will never change," lamented one primary teacher. "We'll always have the standard curriculum and the state tests, won't we?"

A student in a graduate class in school administration agreed with the conclusions of the researchers on grading and grouping but shrugged; "What can we do? If we don't award grades and rank our seniors, the colleges won't accept them and all hell would break loose!" He is partially right. Although most of the research that condemns the impact of the grading and grouping practices in schools was conducted at our universities, these institutions remain bastions of tradition—and certainly nothing is more steeped in tradition than our system of grading and grouping students. But our experience suggests that colleges and universities will work with school districts trying to improve their programs. Imagined resistance to change should not be used as an excuse to avoid facing the defects of our grading and grouping practices.

The schools, the colleges, the state, and the general public are growing increasingly frustrated with attempts to reform a public educational system that is producing too many failed students. The customary remedy has been an intensification of the old practices: toughen up the curriculum, raise the standards, expand the special programs, give more tests. None of these will work. Standing in the way are our practices of grading and grouping. And like the other myths that stymie real school reform in America, the American public and all of its educational subdivisions must confront this reality before bona fide school reform can happen.

Once educational leaders and the public have come to terms with the issue, solutions will spring forth. John Goodlad (1984) suggests a research-based model in *A Place Called School*. The University of California–Santa Cruz, a major research university, eliminated grading years ago. Americans, probably more than any people on earth, are able to accomplish massive changes virtually overnight—once they have clear direction. Grades are not necessary. Far more enlightening reports on the student's progress could be devised than grades if the unrelenting parental pressure to give grades was relaxed.

For the taxpayer, the greatest benefit derived from eliminating the traditional grading and grouping system would be accountability—*true* accountability for learning. America's great testing expertise could be harnessed to develop exhaustive assessment instruments that would comprehensively measure a student's learning—at appropriate times when each individual student is ready to demonstrate mastery. Thus a student's progress through school would be marked by mastery of concepts and skills, not by promotion through age-segregated grades. Teachers would feel free to help all students succeed without worrying about fitting grades to a proper bell curve. Teachers would not be saddled with the schizophrenic job of helping students and at the same time judging them—of being both attorney and judge. Both teacher and student would have the same mission: to master the academic material in order to score well on comprehensive examinations. Parents, teachers, and students would all be on the same side. Master teachers whose students make extraordinary progress would not be chastised for too many As, and weaker teachers would be far less likely to brag about their failures.

More important, the tests would be constructed and administered by testing *specialists*—experts in constructing and administering valid, reliable, authentic test instruments. The potentially life-altering assessments of student progress would no longer be left to chance. Today's practice of allowing students to be tested, sorted, grouped, and graded by virtually untrained amateurs in the field of testing and measurement would end, and professional teachers would be free to concentrate on what they have been prepared to do: teach.

A few of our more cynical colleagues claim that we are simply advocating a Japanese-style testing system. Our response is both yes and no. Yes, we advocate a system that brings together the teacher, family, and student to focus on a common objective and that eliminates the adversarial relationships so common in today's American schools. Yes, we believe in strict accountability for teaching and learning—both for the student and the teacher. But no, we do not believe in closing the door if a student does not master the material by a certain, predetermined point in time. We believe in exploiting the minds of the greatest number of Americans possible and harming as few children as possible in the process.

Testing of the sort described above should not be confused with the national tests or so-called national educational goals being proposed by various groups. Those tests (see Chapter 2) are designed to sample students in age-segregated groups (e.g., third grade) to determine how well the students have learned the "standard" curriculum for that grade—usually a dumbed-down, average-for-the-age course of studies that, as we have discussed, hurts almost all students. The current statewide and nationwide testing movements actually reinforce the crippling practices of grading and grouping that stand in the way of school reform.

The purpose of this discussion is to expose a pernicious and pervasive practice in our public schools that is supported by popular mythology about high academic standards and how children learn. We have suggested how this barrier might be approached, but we will stop short of outlining a full-fledged, K–12 school system. Numerous quality research studies have been conducted to determine which models of schooling best support at-risk students, the gifted, the handicapped, and the so-called regular students. Most of these have enough in common to provide direction. Most don't have a lockstep curriculum, they don't sort students into ability groups, they don't have life-altering negative consequences for failure, and they are all focused on helping students move as fast and as far as they are capable of moving. Sadly, most are not compatible with America's pervasive systems of grading and grouping.

More than thirty years ago, Stanford University banned the issuance of failing grades. Stanford's academic prestige is as great today as it was in 1960. Those who feared the collapse of standards were wrong. Although we do not believe that grading and sorting students at the university level have the same detrimental impact on students that they have in the elementary and secondary schools, a lesson can be learned from the Stanford experience. Moving public education in a truly new direction requires that we dispel the myths and fear surrounding our practices of grading and grouping. The San Diego newspaper editor was right when he stated that failure is a fact of life. Schools, however, must be organized to reinforce success.

Notes

1. An excellent summary of the research regarding the effects of grade retention was compiled by Lorrie Shepard and Mary Lee Smith: "Synthesis of Research on Grade Retention" (cited below); see also "Synthesis of Research on Grouping in Elementary and Secondary Schools," by Robert Slavin, in the September 1988 *Educational Leadership*.

2. For a comprehensive discussion of the history of grading and the myths surrounding grades, see *Grades and Grading Practices*, by Charles Hargis (1990).

References

Goodlad, J. (1984). *A Place Called School*. New York: McGraw-Hill.

Hargis, C. (1990). *Grades and Grading Practices*. Springfield, IL: Charles C Thomas.

Milton, O., H. Pollio, and J. Eisen. (1986). *Making Sense of College Grades*. San Francisco: Jossey-Bass.

San Diego Union. 1991. Board Rates an F. Editorial, 22 July.

Shepard, L., and M. Smith (May 1990). "Synthesis of Research on Grade Retention." *Educational Leadership*.

MYTH 7:
PUBLIC SCHOOLS ARE NOT PERMITTED TO TEACH VALUES

AS LONG AS TESTS ARE ADMINISTERED, THERE WILL ALWAYS BE PRAYER IN SCHOOLS!

Introduction

Cambridge's dean, William Inge, once remarked, "The aim of education is a knowledge not of fact, but of values." Americans desire excellence in their schools but have been strangely unable to come to grips with a simple truth: excellence in our schools is a matter of teaching values. For our students to achieve excellence they must be steeped in the universal values of honesty, responsibility, cooperation, reverence, diligence, kindness, perseverance, and humility. Sound like religion? Perhaps. At least religion and schooling share some common goals. Children who grow and mature in a values-oriented school environment will seek out and embrace *excellence.* This phenomenon was once widely recognized by educators everywhere. Learning can be difficult! At times, it requires fervent, even devout effort. A teacher's mission must be first to prepare the students to learn—to develop self discipline, to find joy in seeking knowledge. Tragically, America's fanatical attempts to keep public education out of the religion business have squelched a primary mission of schools. We do not advocate sectarian religious indoctrination by public schools, but we do believe that it is time to rethink some of the poorly conceived ideas and decisions we've made about teaching values and encouraging religion.

The Myth

It is not unusual these days to hear of a court blocking the use of public funds to maintain a cross in a public park or to construct a manger scene in front of a public office. In most places, school Christmas programs are a thing of the past, and traditional Christmas carols have been replaced by more seasonal songs about snowmen and chestnuts roasting on an open fire. Not long ago, a judge was ordered to remove his copy of the Ten Commandments from his courtroom wall. Even Santa Claus, the consummate symbol of selfless giving, has been summarily expelled from many schools because of his traditional connection with the Christmas celebration—guilt by association! Without a doubt, these court decisions have had a chilling effect on the teaching of values and morals and the healthy discussion of human spirituality in our classrooms. However, we argue that these vital functions of schools have not been outlawed. Educators must recognize this fact and strive to preserve, or in most cases resurrect, the practices. First, though, they must know what they are fighting for.

The separation of church and state as a means to prevent government from imposing state religion and to help guarantee freedom from religious persecution is a venerable tradition and a constitutional guarantee in our country. Until the mid–twentieth century, however, schools were generally viewed more as extensions of the local families than as functions of state government. Consequently, no one raised an eyebrow when moral training was by law a part of the mission of virtually every school in the country—public or private. In those days, teachers and administrators in the public schools were warned not to promote a *specific* religion but rather to promote respect for religions and concepts of morality in general. Because of the makeup of American communities, the Judeo-Christian concepts of morality, in particular, were promoted widely and regularly. School ceremonies often opened with formal prayers. Some public schools even offered optional religious training during the school day, usually sponsored cooperatively by all churches and synagogues in the community at no direct cost to the taxpayers. Those who experienced these weekly religious training programs recall that the freedom to choose training in a particular religion, or to choose not to participate at all, was emphasized. Whether this actually violated the Establishment Clause of the U.S. Constitution is still very questionable in our minds. Unfortunately, whenever these practices were challenged in court, they were not vehemently defended by educational leaders or scholars who understood the eventual undesirable consequences. Rather, educators stood by and watched impotently as one of the most honored aspects of the American public school mission was eroded away beyond recognition.

Blame the Courts?

We underscore the inadequacy of the response from professional educators to the court challenges to make a point about how we got where we are. Our colleagues in educational leadership are quick to fix blame for discipline and morality problems in the schools on the courts. Yet our friends in the judiciary explain that they only make judgments on the arguments presented. They maintain quite correctly that it's up to those who are experts in the dynamics of public schooling to make compelling arguments. We agree. Part of the blame, if not the lion's share, for the mess in our schools begotten by the country's tribunals lies with the leaders of public education.

In the last half-century, the courts have barged into the classrooms and outlawed much of the grace and reverence that traditionally accompanied school programs. Demands to ban prayers in public school graduation exercises have until recently been uniformly supported by the courts. Even seemingly harmless activities like "moments of silence" and elective courses in transcendental meditation have been ruled out on the grounds that these activities *might* have a primary effect of advancing religion. This chapter's cartoon expresses the futility of banning the prayerful expression of hope while questioning the wisdom of the courts' interventions. Since public schools are an arm of the government, the courts surmised, conducting these activities constituted "excessive" governmental entanglement with religion, violating the Establishment Clause of the First Amendment. What the judges failed to recognize, as they led us down this lonesome road, was the chilling effect their decisions would have on the school's mission to help raise decent, caring, ethical human beings—a mission that we now know goes hand-in-hand with academic excellence and intellectual discipline.

After fifty years of this courtroom effluence, a legitimate and widespread concern is developing among Americans about crime, drugs, teen pregnancy, divorce, and other signs of moral deterioration and social collapse. The American culture and nation are faced with a major dilemma in rearing children. Ironically, the doctrine of separation of church and state was originally applied to public schools more to appease anti-Catholic prejudice than to conform with any real constitutional mandates. This quaint interpretation of the First Amendment allowed Protestant-dominated American leaders to block public funds from being appropriated to the Catholic school systems, as they were and are today in Canada. No one ever really doubted that the Canadian government and the Catholic Church were separate enterprises, but the idea that the Catholics would receive taxpayer dollars to support their schools in the United States was galling to the Protestants.[1] It is interesting that the Canadian educators we know agree fully with the church-and-state separation concept. "The Americans," as one British Columbian public school administrator noted concerning the religious ban in U.S. schools, "just got a little carried away."

Traditional Values

Now, panicky cries for a return to "traditional values" are heard. Anti-Catholicism is no longer a major issue, but judges are stuck with the residue of legal precedents that govern their thinking. It could be said that these so-called traditional values are more or less Judeo-Christian in the Anglo-Saxon Protestant tradition. But if we apply common sense, they probably can be more accurately described as universally *American* values and beliefs in the *American tradition*.

Nonetheless, efforts to teach morality and values in public schools continue to be stridently challenged, and educators have been warned by their legal advisers not to impose their values on their students. After all, according to the challengers, America is a pluralistic society, and no one has the right to determine whose values are the right values, even though they usually will grudgingly admit that the same universal human values are embraced by all religions. In Scottsburg, Indiana, a lawyer for the ACLU threatened to sue the school district if it posted what the district called "Common Precepts to Promote a Virtuous and Civil School Community." He claimed the code of moral behavior was unconstitutional because "it suspiciously tracks the Ten Commandments." According to the *New York Times,* the lawyer accused the district of sounding "a bit like Moses" (Johnson, 1999). We say, "So what?"

This paralyzing dilemma, coupled with vague court "tests" and other legal gobbledygook, has caused our school leaders to back away timidly from their crucial roles in the rearing of moral and ethical citizens. Or, worse yet, they resort to simplistic, stultifying programs of Polonius-like exhortations and other drills aimed at making children behave, rather than helping them to learn and embrace the·value structure from which the internal concept of excellence can emerge. For the first time in the history of humankind, a society has eliminated moral and ethical training as the core of its educational system. The pilgrim founders of America's public school tradition would cry out in disbelief. The single purpose of these well-focused pioneer American schools was moral education. Developing one's mind to its fullest was a sacred obligation, and this was the source from whence excellence sprang.

Too Hot to Handle

Educating children with regard to morals and values, so the opponents of values education say, is more properly the role of the church and the family. The public schools should keep their hands off. Some argue that dealing with sensitive social mores in the school setting without the benefit of clear, value-driven moral guidance from the family will create a vacuum that retards character development. For example, when the school declares it will teach sex education, the family feels relieved of the responsibility. The result is even less effective moral guidance to the child than would have been provided had the school stayed out of it.

Others argue that the values education experiments, the so-called character education programs, have been dismal failures and are a waste of the school's time and resources. Critics also point to the dearth of evidence on the effectiveness of character education programs. The time and effort could better be spent on the new primary mission of American schools: teaching self-esteem. "Let's face it," one modern school board member declared, "public schools are not set up to teach morals and manners!" Even though nearly every state's school code requires schools to provide this training, defenders of the no-values approach explain that this is simply a vestigial remnant of a bygone age that has been pre-empted by the courts. "Even if we wanted to, we can't. It's illegal!"

The Reality

Throughout the history of the world, the overarching purpose of education has been to impart the values and mores of a society. As we mentioned before, the architects of the Boston Latin school built their enterprise to accomplish one goal: "to thwart Deluder Satan." The ancient Greeks believed "civic virtue" to be the one overriding purpose for education. Earlier this century, mathematician-philosopher Alfred North Whitehead wrote, "The essence of education is that it be religious. A religious education is an education that inculcates duty and reverence."[2] And according to a recent Public Agenda survey, 71 percent of Americans today say it is more important to teach their kids values than academics.[3]

Court decisions notwithstanding, we say that nothing has changed! Instilling values should still be the central role of the school in the upbringing of our children. Values education involves focusing the mission of the school on a complex pattern for living—synthesized from facts, skills, ethics and principles that are both *learned and practiced*. As Oliver Wendell Holmes declared, "The main part of intellectual education is not the acquisition of facts, but learning how to make facts live."

So if excellent schools have historically focused on values, ethics, and morals, why are American schools dragging their feet? Embracing values education as a central purpose is, after all, nothing more than implementation of the time-honored concept of educating the whole child. By no means does it mean sacrificing basic skills and traditional academics. In fact, as we've discussed above, it means just the opposite. After all, Inge and Holmes were hardly talking about an education deficient in rigorous study and inquiry. Rather, they advocated the conscious inclusion and integration of values in a rigorous but developmentally sound program. Probably most important for America's reform effort, this means espousing a unified purpose for our schools that aims to develop the whole child—a vision of values, ethics, facts, and skills taught as a seamless whole.

When it comes right down to it, there are far more similarities than differences among the world's religions and value systems. The question about whose values are the right values has become moot in communities where researchers have surveyed parents regarding ethical characteristics they hope to see developed in their children. They have found a surprising degree of consensus in communities with varying demographics. In 1994, Public Agenda researchers found that 95 percent of Americans agree that schools should teach racial respect, honesty, and truthfulness. Earlier, child development researchers in northern California found that parents want schools to help them produce children who are (in order of importance) self-confident, dependable, eager to learn, self-directing, cooperative, sensitive, kind, considerate—in other words, the universal ethics and values of humanity.[4] High on everyone's list was eagerness to learn, curiosity about the world, a desire to develop the child's mind to the fullest. The school officials and researchers alike were surprised to find that parents saw self-confidence and dependability as the most important outcomes of a child's upbringing and schooling. Although important, good grades were not the highest priority and certainly were not viewed as the primary mission of the school. Faculty and administrators were also surprised by parental aspirations and support for the school's assistance in the development of value systems within their children.

If no specific religious dogma or rituals are involved, the question of the public school's support of religion need never be raised. Public schools and houses of worship can be mutually supportive in their mission to instill and refine morals, values, and ethics in our youth. This doesn't mean that the practices won't be challenged now and then by antireligion zealots, but we say, "So what?" Our society must rid itself of the belief that schools can't teach morals, manners, ethics, and values. We must fight back in the legislatures and in the courts. Teaching values is not illegal. It's our job.

Unfortunately, most of the recent efforts at installing character education programs in public schools have been ineffective. Much of what passes as values education or character education is junk. The worst are canned programs purchased from publishers and tacked on to the school program. Veteran school administrators usually are not surprised. Creating an "add-on" to address the popular "societal problem du jour" is a standard knee-jerk reaction. Typically, these programs have little school-wide commitment by the faculty. They are usually isolated in a classroom or a unit of study and are not designed to encourage *long-term practice* in moral or ethical behaviors. Nor are they connected to the rest of the school's curriculum and activities. In fact they often have separate instructors. Projects of this sort are actually detrimental to the cause of character education in two ways: First, they irritate teachers by using up valuable time and resources they could be spending on more worthwhile activities; second (and more disturbing), they sidetrack school leaders from investigating the serious research and program development in character education currently being conducted by legitimate researchers.

Contrary to popular belief, good evidence is being collected by reputable researchers that says schools can positively affect the moral behavior of its students. Moreover, long-range studies have demonstrated conclusively that these effects last into adulthood and help shape lives. Data collected over several years from comprehensive, elementary school-based projects designed to teach prosocial behavior demonstrate what can happen when whole schools build their programs around character education. (Solomon, Watson, Delucchi, Schaps, and Battistich, 1988).

The Child Development Project

One example of this is the Child Development Project, a program operated in two largely minority schools in Hayward, a working-class community across the bay from San Francisco, and in five schools in San Ramon, an affluent, mostly white community thirty-five miles east of San Francisco (Kohn, 1990). Twenty-five years ago, two prominent educators wondered whether a research-based program could be developed that would promote what they called "pro-social values and behavior" among school-aged children. The impetus arose out of the criticism developing in the late 1970s that American society was beginning to display an excessive concern with the self and demonstrated a decline in social responsibility and concern for others. Coincidentally, this emerging generation was the first since the landmark court decisions outlawing religion in schools two decades earlier.

Funded by a sizable grant from the William and Flora Hewlett Foundation, researchers devised a comprehensive school intervention program that *integrated* prosocial ethics, values, and behavior with the regular academic program. It was delivered primarily by the classroom teachers but included a schoolwide program and a parent-involvement aspect. Drawing heavily on the research, project directors designed ways to build school and home environments that promoted a healthy moral and ethical balance between concern for self and concern for the rights and needs of others, while maintaining a high level of emphasis on intellectual growth.

Since values and ethics are transmitted both by *what* is taught and *how* it is taught, the program focused on methodology as well as content. Five clusters of program activities emerged: cooperative activities, helping activities, lessons highlighting prosocial values, activities promoting social understanding, and a nonbehaviorist approach to classroom discipline. These five elements were combined with the whole school program and the parent education/home program to produce a comprehensive, pervasive, prosocial environment. The idea was not only to provide increased moral guidance but also to require students to *practice* being more cooperative, more helpful, more understanding, and more considerate and well-behaved. Values and ethics again became a major part of the basic mission of the schools. The language arts program for every grade was based in a carefully selected collection of "prosocial" literature. Thus, a part of each day was spent discussing ethics and morality in literary as well as historical situations, emphasizing the role of ethical and moral systems as the bases for life decisions. Students also discussed and practiced these various virtues as part of math instruction, as part of recess games, as part of schoolwide projects, as a part of family homework activities with parents, and as a part of "buddy" programs and field activities. In other words, values and ethics became a truly integral part of school (Streshly and Schaps, 1988).

The data collected by staff researchers over the years convincingly proved that integrated prosocial character education is feasible. Repeated observations were initially conducted each year for five years to assess students' interpersonal behavior in three program schools and three comparison schools. Analyses of these data indicated significantly more positive student behavior in the classroom. To no one's surprise, the students also performed as well or better academically.

Other Programs

In Luchow, India, the City Montessori School built its program around the teachings of Mahatma Gandhi. The primary mission was to teach the principles of unity of humankind and universal brotherhood. Beginning with preschool, classroom experience centered around the following four ethics-laden concepts:

- *Universal values*—very similar to the Child Development Project described above;
- *Excellence*—which, according to observers of the school, is a natural consequence of the values focus;
- *Global understanding*—which is a value concept built on the preceding two; and
- *Service*—the commitment to make the world a better place—which is another natural consequence of the values focus.

How does this school fare academically? Its students outscore *all* other Indian schools on national and state-level high school board exams. Its record of merit scholarships and other honors is unmatched by any Indian school (Cottom, 1996). We were particularly interested to find that an amazing 99 percent of the school's students maintain an average grade of *A* and that an equally amazing 99 percent graduate from high school (compared to 30 percent in the state overall). These data support dramatically our arguments about grading and grouping myths.

In northern Europe, Waldorf Education has become very popular. In West Germany, more than 5 percent of all children in the country now attend a school using Waldorf's values-oriented approach. The motto on the Waldorf Association's brochure proclaims, "When the intellect travels on wings of goodness, beauty, and truth, it can reach new heights!" Waldorf schools are also catching on in the United States. According to one analyst, "One reason is that many baby boomer parents appreciate the spiritual values the Waldorf schools espouse." It is interesting to note that Waldorf Schools are now the largest and fastest-growing nonsectarian educational movement in the world.

The Solution

The notion that schools in America cannot legally teach ethics and values for fear of attracting swarms of lawyers promoting lawsuits over religion in the schools has been exaggerated in the minds of public school leaders. True, the fear is not entirely unfounded. Much of the law is hazy and unsettled. Prominent attorneys specializing in this area admit the court decisions have been at best confusing and at worst unintelligible. We believe judicial confusion and lack of clarity, more than any real constitutional problem, create this barrier to school reform. The values-based programs described above demonstrate the vital importance of this reform to our country. America must not allow another generation of its citizens to graduate without substantial education in morals, values, and ethics. What's more, these programs demonstrate that it can be done in the face of adversity. In India, the City Montessori School encountered resistance from parents and the community objecting to their children being taught universal values from the world's religions. In America, the Child Development Project conducted its program ever mindful of the possibility of attack by opponents of values education. Both overcame these problems through the creation of strong programs and old-fashioned hard work and persistence.

It is also important to educate the legal establishment on the importance of rethinking the tack taken over the last half-century. Does school sponsorship of high school baccalaureate ceremonies or any of the community customs associated with religion really constitute an "excessive" entanglement of government and religion? Are schools really an "arm of the government" in the sense envisioned by the framers of the U.S. Constitution? Would financial support for church-affiliated schools really be a violation of the First Amendment? We don't think that the GI Bill, which allowed public funds to be funneled into church-sponsored colleges, constituted government sponsorship of religion. It is time for the judiciary to pause and take stock. Any widespread reform will eventually need the support of the courts to work.

For now, it's up to the leaders of individual schools and districts to rid themselves of the myth surrounding values education and take the initiative. The key elements are as follows:

- Garner parent support for the values education project well in advance. Survey parents regarding their hopes, fears, and aspirations for their children. Survey parents to see what they want for their children from the school. Then school the parents on what works and involve them in the planning.
- Design a *pervasive* schoolwide program, incorporating it as part of *every* lesson, *every* subject. The Child Development Project, the Waldorf Schools, and the Montessori Schools have excellent ideas about how to do this. Activities include whole school interactions, school beautification projects, theme assemblies, grandparents day, and other schoolwide programs.
- Put a heavy emphasis on teaching about virtue, compassion, and helpfulness. Devise activities that promote these virtues and require students to practice them. These include cross-age "buddy" programs, schoolwide responses to disasters in the news, newcomer welcoming programs, visits to convalescent homes for holiday singing or other entertainment, child or family adoption projects, and other human outreach programs.
- Emphasize the virtue of excellence in all endeavors.
- Create a strong, well maintained home link. This means every teacher as well as the front office must be on board and committed to the program. Family homework, family heritage day, parent service projects, cooperative family projects—all can play a significant role in bringing the family into the school.

Whether we consciously make it a part of the official curriculum or not, our students are constantly learning how the world works and how they will interact with the people in it. Through their small eyes and ears passes the data necessary for them to formulate their ethical and moral codes. Schools have historically played a significant major role in this process, and as we have explained above, excellence in education requires a values approach. Lamentably, this role has been diminished in America's schools over the past few decades by well-meaning judges and school administrators who did not fully understand the devastating long-range social implications. Meaningful school reform must include a renewed dedication to helping our children grow into humane and principled adults.

Notes

1. Myron Lieberman discusses the anti-Catholic social dynamics in the 1840s leading to widespread support of nonsectarian public schools, beginning with "A Historical Note," on page 14 of *Public Education: An Autopsy* (Cambridge: Harvard University Press, 1993). He cites Lloyd Jorgenson (*The State and the Non-Public School*, Columbia: University of Missouri Press, 1987) and others in his argument that public nonsectarian schools resulted primarily from "Protestant dissatisfaction with nonpreferential assistance to Catholic schools." Lieberman goes on to say, "The notion that our founding fathers viewed public education as the way to educate citizens about the great issues of the day is preposterous." In his view, nonsectarian education's "raison d'etre was religious prejudice, not the need to educate all children."

2. For a discussion of this point of view in today's setting, read Denis Doyle's "Education and Character: A Conservative View" (cited below). Doyle maintains that schools that serve a heterogeneous population are properly nonsectarian, but they cannot ignore religion.

3. Public Agenda's report entitled *First Things First: What Americans Want from the Public Schools* (Johnson and Immerwahr, 1994) (cited below) describes ten research findings from a survey of Americans that have implications for school reform.

4. Researchers from the Child Development Center (now located in Oakland, California) kicked off an experimental values education project in the San Ramon Valley (California) Unified School District by surveying parents. The program and results of their research are reported in the winter 1988 volume of the *American Educational Research Journal* (vol. 25, no. 4, pp. 527–554) in a report entitled, "Enhancing Children's Prosocial Behavior in the Classroom."

References

Cottom, C. "A Bold Experiment in Teaching Values." *Educational Leadership* (May 1996).

Doyle, D. "Education and Character: A Conservative View." *Phi Delta Kappan* (February 1997).

Johnson, D. "School Creates Its Own Commandments and Fuss." *New York Times*, December 10, 1999, p. A23.

Johnson, J., and J. Immerwahr. (1994). *First Things First: What Americans Want from the Public Schools*. New York: Public Agenda.

Kohn, A. "The ABC's of Caring." *Teacher Magazine* (January 1990).

Schaps, Solomon, D., M. Watson, K. Delucchi, E. Schaps, and V. Battistich. "Enhancing Children's Prosocial Behavior in the Classroom." *American Educational Research Journal* (Winter 1988).

Streshly, W., and E. Schaps. "Let's Help Children Grow into Humane and Principled Adults." *American School Boards Journal* (November 1988).

MYTH 8:
TEACHER EVALUATION ENSURES HIGH-QUALITY INSTRUCTION

Introduction

School districts in every U.S. state are required by law to evaluate teachers. In each state, the written legislative purpose of the evaluations is to ensure that all American youths are taught by competent teachers. If com-

petency is questionable, the evaluation should be accompanied with recommendations intended to bring about improvement. With few excep-
tions, the 11,000 school districts in the United States comply with state
law. What we found is that this compliance is extremely limited, generally
to completing the paperwork requirements of the law, not the spirit and
intent. The proper forms are filled out, but with incorrect information.
The goal of improving teaching is seldom addressed, let alone achieved
(Frase & Streshly, 1994).

Since 1990, we and other auditors conducting curriculum management
audits reviewed a 10 percent random sample of 400,000 teacher evaluations in many school districts across the United States. The makeup of the
districts varied: inner city, urban, rural, wealthy, poor, large, and small
districts serving students of all races, creeds, and ethnic groups. The auditors conducted brief observations in the vast majority of *all* classrooms in
these districts.

The Myth

The myth is threefold:

- The results of the evaluations are accurate.
- Legislative requirements for teacher evaluation ensure the public that
  only good teachers are in classrooms. The evaluations lead to improved instruction.
- School principals are adequately trained to conduct high-quality
  teacher evaluations and offer legitimate suggestions for improvement.

Our study of the teacher evaluations found that nearly all teachers were
rated good to excellent. A sample taken from the Zeus School District
Curriculum Management Audit (see chapter 4) is illustrative. The percentages are based on the total number of teachers evaluated—3,941.
Thirty-two percent, 2,104, of the teachers were not evaluated even though
board policy required at least one formal observation yearly per teacher.
The following results were tallied: 88 percent—Very Good or Outstanding; 12 percent—Adequate; 0 percent—Conditional or Unsatisfactory.
Similar results were found for evaluations of school principals—85 percent outstanding and 15 percent incomplete evaluations.

What could be better news? Education is the key to our national success. High-quality teachers educate our young and provide the foundation for our great democracy. (We are quick to note that our reviews of

administrator evaluations reveal the same distribution of ratings.) In reality, our research and that of others (Bridges, 1986) show that 5 to 20 percent of teachers are incompetent. This idea is gaining exposure, and that is good news. The *New York Times* (Lewin, 1997) ran a story about a teacher whose methods were quite suspect. When observed by an administrator, the teacher's students were often "asleep while the teacher sat reading the paper and drinking coffee, his feet on the desk, shoes off." This teacher was in his first year at the school, but he had tenure and twenty-five years in the district. He had been danced from one school to the next, in the "dance of the lemons." Finally, after failing to improve after receiving two years of professional assistance (seventy-five observations and twenty-nine conferences) from fellow teachers, he was suspended without pay. But the case is not finished; he is of a minority racial group, as is his principal, and has filed a federal suit claiming racial discrimination.

Why do teachers such as these (and others we discuss later) remain in classrooms? The bottom line is that school administrators have generally given up. The Grossmont Union High School District near San Diego spent $500,000 in legal fees over a decade in an attempt to dismiss a teacher. The documentation on the teacher's performance was clear; in her classes, the students simply sat chattering, reading letters, looking at nonclass-related books, or just sat, waiting for the period to end. Teachers complained about her, students signed petitions, administrators compiled undeniable documentation, but it took years, $500,000, and thousands of hours of administrative time to dismiss her. As Mary Jo McGrath, a top-flight attorney, said, "Dismissing an incompetent teacher makes the O.J. [Simpson] case look like a cakewalk" (Lewin, 1997).

The belief that teaching is excellent has rubbed off on the American public; national polls show that parents and other community members believe that teachers and administrators in their local schools are doing a fine job.

The Reality

The fact is that our and other auditors' observations in Zeus School District (a large urban district) and many other districts revealed that 80 percent of the teaching observed was at worst horrible and less than mediocre at best. The laissez-faire attitude shrouded disastrous teaching in firm statements of excellence. Here is how auditors commonly described classroom activities and teaching.

- Low-level thinking (cognition) activities: copying words from the board and writing definitions from the dictionary; copying directions

and questions from workbooks and textbooks; and doing work-
sheets. Dynamic, exciting, and challenging lessons that required sophisticated thinking were rare.

- Teachers sitting and not engaged with the students: reading newspaper, grading papers, talking on phone, and working on bulletin-
  board displays. In other words, not teaching.
- Large percentages of students off-task—looking out windows, talking, walking around room, and some sleeping. In other words, not
  learning the material or developing the skills they should.
- In secondary schools class started three to ten minutes after the bell,
  and class ended three to ten minutes before the bell.
- No teachers in classrooms full of students.[1]

We want to make it abundantly clear that we did find some isolated
examples of excellent teaching; unfortunately, there were few and far between.

The Lake Woebegone phenomenon exists in education. Everyone is
great. As in Lake Woebegone, the phenomenon of "all is well and good"
is a myth. So how can we account for these woefully incorrect percep-
tions?

First, teaching is a helping profession. Hence, the propensity for saying
nice things only to fellow workers is rampant. However, when asked in
private if they were aware of any incompetent or marginal teachers in
their schools, nearly 100 percent of the principals, teachers, parents, and
executive administrators said yes. The percentages identified ranged
from 1 percent to 25 percent, even though excellent or good ratings were
assigned in the evaluations. So why the striking contrast between these
percentages and the official evaluation ratings given teachers? The answers are varied, creative, and depressing.

- In the Zeus School District some of the principals said that the
  teacher contract prohibited them from giving low performance ratings. They also said that the contract limited the number of unan-
  nounced visits or observations they could conduct in classrooms.
  This proved to be a red herring. We read the contract, and it con-
  tained *no* such restrictions. In fact, it gave evaluators much leeway to
  accomplish high-quality evaluations.
- Many school principals' decisions regarding evaluation are influenced by their humanistic spirit. For example, they said that they
  "felt sorry for the teacher"; "the teacher was really trying"; "the
  teacher had serious problems at home"; or that "the teacher did a

good job on playground supervision and volunteered for many com-
mittees so overlooked the teaching."

- In many districts teachers told us that they are asked to sign their
written evaluation without the principal ever conducting an observation.
- Politics intervene to hide the truth. None of these are acceptable substitutes for ensuring that every student has a competent teacher.
These reveal that the district goes through the motions of filling out
the forms in order to meet state legal requirements. But the intended
purpose of improving performance is not taken seriously. The laissez-faire attitude of "just fill out the forms" is pervasive.

Politics is the most insidious element. Examples range from isolated
cases in which a principal is told by a board member or the superintendent not to pursue stringent evaluation procedures with a teacher because "he is a friend and a good person." The principal is left with a feck-
less response to complaining parents—"We are working on it"—when in
fact the only thing the district is working on is covering up the teachers'
incompetence while thirty students suffer daily. We found these cases in
many districts we audited. In one case, 80 percent of the employees in a
school were relatives of the principal or board members and could not
teach. Another case in point popped up in a *New York Times* editorial
about Connetquot School District (No Author, 1997). Local residents had
complained about the qualifications of teachers, especially those whose
relatives were school board members when they were hired. To investi-
gate qualifications, the district required all 758 applicants to take a Regents test normally given to high school juniors. The test comprised fifty
multiple-choice, reading comprehension questions. Surprisingly, only
202 of the applicants passed the test. That's right, a test intended for high
school juniors. This is appalling.[2]

Events in Large City School District (a very large urban district) offer
an example on a grand scale. We toured a random sample of forty schools
and read a 10 percent random sample of teacher evaluations for two
school years. The tours of schools and the analysis of the evaluations revealed astonishingly opposite findings. Teaching and classroom activities,
as stated earlier, lacked luster and excitement. They were inept, passive,
and boring. More important, students were not challenged or engaged.
But teacher evaluations generally rated teachers as very good or excellent.

One example is particularly telling. The audit team found that in secondary schools most teachers started class five to ten minutes after the
bell rang and finished five to ten minutes before the final bell rang. Most
schedules called for the classes to be fifty minutes long, and the district

claimed that students spent 180 days in school (see Chapter 9). Here is the tragedy. When classes begin five minutes late and end five minutes early, students lose ten minutes of instruction in each class. So instead of fifty minutes, the period is only forty minutes. Considering a 180-day school year and a seven-period day, the students in these classes were deprived of thirty-five six-hour days of schooling. The effect is that the 180-day school year shrinks to 145 days. When the classes begin ten minutes late and end ten minutes early, the number of days is reduced to 110. The highly touted 180-day school year is a sham. When asked why classes were so short, many principals did not respond; others said, "That's the way it is," and a few said, "I've told them to stick to the schedule." As though this is not sufficiently appalling, the story gets more pathetic.

How do politics fit in? The state comptroller's office was in charge of administering this review, and the team members were required to submit findings and recommendations to the office throughout the process. The results stated in the last paragraph were discussed many times with the comptroller's administrators and were presented to fifty Large City School District administrators. At a later date we arrived in Large City School District to do our part in reporting our team's findings at a press conference. In a private meeting with and in front of other team leaders, the comptroller's administrator informed us that we were not going to give our report on education and curriculum. She said that it had been rewritten and one of their staff members would give it. Further, she said, we would give our other report on personnel, but nothing should be said about any of the findings regarding the poor quality of teaching supervision or anything else not in the "rewritten" report. This was certainly a blow—to our purpose in being there, to our integrity, and most important to the chances of improving education for the students in Large City School District. Indeed, this case even expands the cast of actors in what Ted Sizer called a "conspiracy of the least," a tacit agreement between teachers and students to do just enough to get by. The state office was also participating in covering up the truth.

For certain, teachers and principals are not fully to blame for poor teaching. We asked districts for a list of training programs provided to principals. We are looking for training in using a variety of research-proven teaching methods and training in analyzing classroom interaction and instruction. We most frequently find that *no* training is given to principals to better enable them to conduct teacher evaluation. We also asked principals to tell us when they last received training in conducting teacher evaluations. Many say they can't remember the last training or that they have no recollection. Those that do remember say anywhere from "last year" to "eight years ago." Last year isn't bad, no? *NO!* What we found was that the training they referred to was cursory or not directly related to instruction. Frequently the training was procedural only (e.g., time lines, how to fill out forms).[3]

Many states provide training for principals before allowing principals to conduct teacher evaluations. But monitoring of the quality of the evaluations is absent in most districts. For the principal the implications are obvious—no need to see the teacher; just fill out the form and file it.

The Solution

The solution is quite simple and straightforward. First and foremost, we must not succumb to more airy-fairy grand reforms like restructuring, site-based management, and the like. What is needed is high-quality instruction and administration. The following actions will result in improved education:

- Legislators in each state work with school board, teacher, and administrator associations to reduce due-process requirements for teacher dismissal to a reasonable level, one that doesn't protect the incompetent. State legislators such as Florida, Oregon, and New York have instituted legislative changes to do just that.
- School boards state publicly and widely that top-notch instruction is required.
- Boards create policy that says that principals must take time to work with teachers in classrooms and evaluate them to bring about further improved teaching.
- Boards budget money each year and require the administration to provide high-quality training in improving classroom teaching. Boards budget money each year and require that administrators seek and take high-quality training each year in analyzing classroom interaction, teaching, developing improvement plans for teachers and themselves, and participating with teachers in teacher training.
- Boards direct the superintendent to develop work plans that allow principals plenty of time to be in classrooms working with and observing teachers and writing evaluation reports and improvement plans. This may mean eliminating less valuable duties such as developing select reports, spending less time in the office, and reducing the number of meetings.
- School boards agree to have highly rigorous and objective curriculum

management audits performed every year. This will elevate the importance of curriculum and teaching to that of finance—where the state requires an audit every year for every school district (Frase, English, and Poston, 1994; English, 1999).

- Boards direct the superintendent to develop a series of criteria for assessing the impact of each of these actions and make quarterly reports to the board.

These actions are not fancy. They are basic, and that is what is needed. Teaching is the most influential factor in our children's formal education. Research data overwhelmingly say that high-quality teaching results in more learning than poor-quality teaching. We know that schools were never intended to be halfway houses for incompetent teachers or administrators. So we query, "What here is not clear?" The need for high-quality teaching is as clear as the need for education itself.

Notes

1. For studies in this area see Bridges (1986) and Frase and Streshly (1994).

2. A study also found that in schools with the lowest third-grade reading scores on the SAT-9, 22 percent of the teachers were underqualified. In contrast, schools in which just 4 percent of teachers were underqualified had the highest scores. Further, more than 1 million of the state's 5.7 million students attend schools with "so many underqualified teachers as to make these schools dysfunctional" (Bradley, 1999). It is important to note that many of these teachers are working with "emergency" credentials and have not completed university training.

3. For further reading on the topic of how school organizations are greatly responsible for poor teaching, see Frase and Conley (1994), Sarason (1990), Van Horn (1999), and Schalock, Schalock, and Myton (1998).

References

Bradley, A. (1999). " 'Quality' Crisis Seen in Calif. Teaching Ranks." *Education Week* 19, no. 10, p. 1.

Bridges, E. (1986). *The Incompetent Teacher*. Philadelphia: Falmer Press.

English, F. (1999): *Deciding What to Teach & Test*. Thousand Oaks, CA: Corwin Press.

Frase, L., and S. Conley. (1994). *Creating Learning Places for Teachers, Too*. Thousand Oaks, CA: Corwin Press.

Frase, L., and W. Streshly. (1994). "Lack of Accuracy, Feedback, and Commitment in Teacher Evaluation." *Journal of Personnel Evaluation in Education.*

Frase, L., F. English, and W. Poston. (1994) *The Curriculum Management Audit.* Lanham, MD: Scarecrow Press.

Lewin, T. (1997). "New Methods Tested in Response to Teachers Who Fail to Teach." *New York Times* (vol. 146, no. 50,875), section A p. 1.

No Author (1997). "Student Hurdle Foils Teachers," *New York Times* (vol. 146, no. 50,847), p. A12

Sarason, S. (1990). *The Predictable Failure of School Reform.* San Francisco: Jossey-Bass.

Schalock, D., M. Schalock, and D. Myton. (1998). Effectiveness—Along with Quality—Should Be the Focus." *Phi Delta Kappan* 79(6), p. 468.

Sizer, T. (1992). *Horace's School: Redesigning the American High School.* Boston: Houghton Mifflin Company.

Van Horn, R. (1999). "Inner-city Schools: A Multiple-Variable Discussion." *Phi Delta Kappan* 81(4), p. 291.

MYTH 9:
MERIT PAY FOR TEACHERS IS
UNETHICAL AND CANNOT WORK

Introduction

A wise person once said that there is nothing so unequal as treating un-
equals equally. Somehow this wisdom has escaped the people responsi-

ble for setting teachers' and principals' salaries. We have asked hundreds of principals, teachers, and parents if some teachers in their school are better at their craft than others. Without exception, all said "yes." Most said that some teachers are much better than others, some are excellent, and some are really not very good at all. Boldly, many said some are incompetent. Educational literature is full of evidence that the quality of teaching between and within schools varies from very bad to very good. So, one would reasonably think that people who perform better would receive higher pay. Right? Wrong! Teacher pay is based on the single-salary schedule, a plan of Paleolithic vintage.

The Myth

The myth is that teaching cannot be assessed or measured. Education is so complex that no person can judge its quality; the product is simply too different. Defenders of this myth argue that teacher pay cannot and should not be based on quality of teaching. Unlike those who work with the automobile, toaster, popcorn popper, or the infamous widgets produced on the assembly line, the defenders say that teachers work with young minds. This myth is based on three equally fallacious assumptions: quality of teaching cannot be judged; legitimacy of the single-salary schedule; and using student achievement to assess teaching is immoral. Each is discussed below.

Underlying Assumption No. 1: You Can't Make Quality Judgments about Teaching

Purveyors of this assumption argue that merit pay is stupid and impossible. Why? For them, the answer is obvious: basing pay on observations of their classroom work is also impossible. They say there are too many uncontrollable variables to base pay on student achievement. Teachers must apply their skills within the classroom context of what is to be learned and what each student brings to the classroom, including prior achievement, socioeconomic status, physical condition, and whatever is on the student's mind. Teachers are with the students every day. How could anyone, based on one or ten observations, truly judge the quality of teaching? Teaching must be personalized; it cannot be defined by a list of teacher behaviors or classroom characteristics. Teaching is more than just a random, or even orderly, concatenated assemblage of behaviors. Each classroom and group of students requires something different. The most appropriate teaching methods, verbal and nonverbal communication, and behaviors are totally dependent on context. It is holistic and so on. In other words, solid, accurate evaluation of teaching by an observer is impossible.

Based on these assertions, merit pay is foolhardy, and anyone thinking the contrary just doesn't know teaching. Merit pay is a diabolical myth foisted upon teachers by atomistic-minded administrators, school board members, and business people. Further, it is nearly impossible to assess the act of teaching. (These people overgeneralize the validity of one of postmodernism's basic tenets—indeterminacy—and use it to squelch a priori reasoning such as making assumptions about good and bad teaching. Postmodernists know that one cannot *know* because change is continuous and is defined by context. A job as complex as teaching defies definition of standards of quality. They claim, "It all depends.") Both students and teachers suffer as a result of merit pay. Merit pay may be right in industry, but not in teaching. Teaching and school administration are different.

Underlying Assumption No. 2: The Single-Salary Schedule Is the Best and Right Way

Those who cling to this myth argue that basing teacher and administrator pay on their years of experience and postgraduate training makes sense. Teachers get better with each year of experience and with the graduate credit; so do principals. The schedule holds the profession together and protects it from unjust salary determinations of gormless administrators.

Each school district in the United States, with the exception of Hawaii, has its own salary schedule for teachers and principals, and they vary in dollars, but nearly all use only years of experience and postgraduate training as the criteria for determining pay. This means, for example, that all teachers in a school district with five years of teaching experience plus a masters degree and ten additional hours of graduate credit receive the same pay. Hence, teachers with the same graduate training and number of years of experience receive the same pay. One, two, or twenty teachers may have equal training and experience. They also have equal pay. This is the moral high ground, the professional way to do it (see the cartoon). Why? Supporters of the single-salary schedule assert that teachers are required to have the equivalent training; they teach pretty much the same number of hours each day. They further claim that all teachers and principals work hard, teach equally well, and are professionals. They get better with each year of experience and each graduate training hour, so the pay should be equal. Supporters of this assumption believe that this is the path to equality.

Underlying Assumption No. 3: Using Student Achievement to Assess Teaching Is Immoral

Some public activists, teachers, and school administrators profess that standardized testing (e.g., SAT, ACT, and the Iowa Test of Basic Skills) is philosophically wrong in the first place, to say nothing of its total illegitimacy as a measure of quality. Proponents of the myth claim that these tests sample only a small portion of what the students need to learn, and in teaching this the curriculum is narrowed to a bare sliver of what needs to be learned. Further, backers of this assumption claim that teaching to the test may increase test scores, but it only serves the egos of the superintendents and board members who in turn brag about their accomplishments.

Some go so far as to say that teaching to the test is dishonest. It is ethically corrupt. If you teach to the test it is no longer a test. Call it review or practice, but not a test. *Based on this, obviously* the test must be kept a secret from the students in order to measure their achievement accurately.

This ill-conceived belief underlies many myths in education (see Chapter 6).

The Reality

Opponents of merit pay are tenacious; they have won their way with each merit-pay plan.[1] Hundreds have come and gone over the past ninety years. Therefore, teachers or principals in the same school district with the same number of graduate training hours and the same number of years of experience continue to receive identical pay. That's the way it is. Raises are received with each year of experience and as graduate training hours are collected.[2]

Rejoinder: You Can Make Quality Judgments about Teaching

The notion that good teaching just happens, that it is unpredictable and cannot be known beforehand, is ludicrous. No profession approaches its clients with such muddled indeterminacy. From the far less complex automotive mechanic to the neurosurgeon, professionals know what to look for, how to judge it when they see it, and, finally, what to do to correct problems. Physicians have an array of possible treatments as they diagnose an illness; they know that depending on the condition, some work better than others do. We dare say that you would not return to your doctor if he or she simply prescribed the same medicine to all patients regardless of the illness. Consider sitting in the dentist's chair and, as he or she walks in, he or she says, "I pulled a tooth from each of the last four patients, so I'll do the *same* for you. *Please open your mouth widely.*" Instead, doctors and dentists diagnose and then treat. Logical? Yes! The typical protocol is to diagnose, treat, assess effects, and, if necessary, to diagnose and treat again.

Research over the past thirty-five years is clear about effective teaching practices. It is not a mystery. Some teaching techniques and educational practices result in more learning than other techniques. It's as simple as that. Witness the plethora of research on direct instruction, academic learning time (ALT), and cooperative learning. These even make common sense. For example, in direct instruction, teaching students specific skills and information is more effective than teaching them a little about what they need to know plus some other stuff that is irrelevant to what they are to learn. We say teaching students what you want them to learn makes sense. Also consider increasing ALT. It makes sense that spending more time actually teaching and engaging students in study results in higher achievement than not. We ask rhetorically, "Is this rocket science?" We don't think so.

Analyses of classroom videotapes from the Third International Mathematics and Science Study (Stigler, 1997) strongly support these common-sense strategies and provide even further clarification. They measure *the tendencies of* countries and school districts to specify what students are to learn (curriculum) and the amount and percentage of time teachers devote to it. They found that having a highly specific curriculum and devoting all class time to teaching it resulted in more learning than that in classrooms where students do other things, like having the last fifteen minutes of class to start their homework. Students of countries and school districts producing high achievement levels do their homework at *home*, not school. Complicated? Mysterious? No. Make sense? Yes.

We have been appalled with the instruction as we walk through some classrooms, especially in schools where the majority of students is African American. In Large City School District, up to one-third of class time in the schools studied was lost due to starting class late and ending early. In our curriculum management audits of five large inner-city schools, we witnessed bored, inactive classes where students were doing anything but learning and teachers were doing anything but teaching. Indeed, this is another example of the "conspiracy of the least"—the tacit agreement between teachers and students to do just enough to get by.

The quality of teaching *can* be judged accurately. The literature clearly shows educators what teaching methods work best, in what conditions, and when. Research results will continue to evolve. It is probably true that the artful nature of teaching cannot be defined by scientific methods. To do so would eliminate that nature of a very complex activity. However, the research base comparing some techniques with others is strong and should not be ignored. At this time most educators are not aware of them, and only a few are using them to further enhance their artful skills and thereby increase student achievement.

Rejoinder: The Single-Salary Schedule Is Obsolete and Fosters Mediocrity

That the quality of teaching necessarily improves with experience and additional training is truly a myth. Mounds of research rail against this assumption. Although we would like to think it is true, years of experience and additional training frequently do not necessarily result in improved teaching. In fact, numerous studies show that teaching performance plateaus and begins to decline anywhere from the second to the seventh year. Research also exists showing that university graduate training and training provided by school districts also do not result in improved teaching (Bridge, 1979). In fact, there is no correlation between teachers' experience or education level and principals' and parents' assessment of teaching quality (Epstein, 1985)—quite the opposite of the assumptions underlying the single-salary schedule.

As many salary schedule reformers have found, the single-salary schedule has seemingly invincible inertia. The first pay-for-performance plan was tried in England around 1710 and was drubbed out by a group of protesters claiming that it resulted in the "cult of the [cash] register" where teachers no longer cared about children, just pay (Wilms and Chapleau, 1999). Since the nineteenth century in the United States, reformers have attempted to add quality of performance to the salary formula. As early as 1867, Aaron Sheeley, superintendent of Adams County, Pennsylvania, lamented the injustices of compensation systems that required the same pay for all teachers without recognition of performance. In 1958, Clarence Haines, superintendent of schools in Eugene, Oregon, wrote this bias into the literature by saying that compensation based on performance is basic to the American system and that the public is opposed to paying average or mediocre teachers as much as it pays superior teachers. In 1983 President Reagan echoed this call for "Americanization" of teachers' pay when he, in the famous *A Nation at Risk* (1983) report, said that our schools would be better if we paid our best teachers more than our worst. The past ninety years have witnessed many alternative pay plans. Many came, some stayed a while, and all failed to win long-term teacher support. This myth is not necessarily held by American society but instead is a seemingly religious tenet of most teachers and teacher associations.

Rejoinder: Student Achievement Is a Proper Measure of Teaching

Why would anyone think that teaching *to* the test is wrong for any reason? Students must be taught the skills and concepts they are expected to learn and that will be on the test. To us, not teaching the skills required by a test is malpractice. We can't imagine it. Would we not be outraged to sit through a class and then be tested on something that was not taught? You bet we would. And we were. We sat through university sociology and numerous graduate education classes wondering what the instructors thought they were teaching. Certainly it was a mystery to us. The tests and the grading criteria didn't match up.[3]

Now, we know that teaching the exact test items is wrong (see Chapter 2 regarding national standards). That is teaching the test. The test items are simply a sampling of the skills, knowledge, and applications they are designed to assess. When teaching *the* test, students could learn the items but be ignorant of the underlying concepts. Teaching the exact items is also malpractice and renders the test useless and encourages ignorance. But let's get real: if you want kids to learn something, does it not make good sense to teach it to them? Of course it does. Moreover, we condemn the self-aggrandizing politicians who use test scores for political gain. These political opportunists differentiate between various groups to create demonic bogeymen that they can exorcise from the educational institution. This silly practice gains votes. A high-quality, well-aligned testing program in the hands of professionals can result in big learning gains. As discussed in Chapter 2, we do not confuse these programs with the politically driven national standards and testing movements that are designed to assign blame.

Part of the myth is that superintendents and board members just want high test scores for their political benefit. First, we doubt that, since we were superintendents for twenty-five years. Second, the desired political benefit is a natural result of student achievement. Many educators, politicians, and most taxpayers want higher achievement. To give consumers what they want is not dishonest. It is good practice.

Those who argue against the use of learning as a means of determining pay levels say that there are too many uncontrolled variables to allow legitimate linkage between learning and pay. Yes, there are variables that make it difficult, but our conversations with industrial leaders and managers reveal that subjectivity plays a role in determining salaries in industry also. We have found no industrial leader claiming a wholly objective scheme for determining pay. Total objectivity is a myth.

When we demystify education, realize that we do know what good teaching is, admit that teaching *to* the test is proper, and that the single-salary schedule is folderol leading to educational mediocrity, all of a sudden merit pay sounds good and possible.

Easy, no! But what is? Here are our suggestions.

The Solution

Background

The overarching and most important change in philosophy is to get the benefits and effects of internal and external rewards straight. First, the need for external rewards or pay is obvious. Everyone needs money to exist.[4] In the world economy, adequate amounts of money allow people to live without immediate threat to their basic psychological welfare. No startling news there! However, the well-known but seldom admitted truth is that more money is no guarantee to happiness; in fact, it is frequently a deterrent. Once basic needs such as salary, insurance, and security are covered, intrinsic rewards become the most powerful sources of motivation and satisfaction. That is simply the way it is.[5]

We show in Chapter 3 that teacher and administrator unions and school boards focus almost totally on extrinsic rewards. Somehow, they cling to the belief that giving a bit more money will win greater goodwill, esprit de corps, happiness, and better work from the employees. So both sides end up haggling and creating ill will over tiny fractions of percentage increases in salary. The envisioned effect is illusory. Unless salaries are below basic levels, raises result in none of these. Bok's (1993) analysis of research studies in this area is profound.[6] He tells us that even though Americans' real income is more than twice as much now than in the 1950s, they express no greater satisfaction. Wealthier Americans express considerably less satisfaction now than they did then. Some studies that show a correlation between income and happiness clearly state that the effect of affluence on happiness is dwarfed by the impact of blessings that money cannot buy, such as friends, good health, and warm family relationships.

So after all the haggling of a few tenths of a percent pay increase, there may be some high-fiving to celebrate the victory, but the thrill passes quickly. Pay raises historically have very short effect on anything other than reinforcing the ill-conceived drive to get more. Over the past fifty years, research literature in private industry is packed with evidence that money, at best, even in large amounts, results in only short-term productivity gains and that the most powerful source of motivation is successfully completing valued work.[7] The same wisdom has been espoused repeatedly over the centuries by scholars and philosophers such as Chuang Tzu, Tao, Saint Thomas Aquinas, Henri Bergson, and the authors of *Bhagavad Gita*. For centuries these people have advised that doing one's work well is inextricably linked to quality of life. As Thomas Aquinas said, "To work well is to live well." More recently, the writings of Vaclav Havel (1991), Paul Davies (1995), Rupert Sheldrake (1994), Mihaly Csikszentmihalyi (1990), Michael Fox (1994), and Scott Peck (1995) arrived at the same, or very similar, conclusion. The case is even more true for helping professions such as teaching.

So what do financial rewards really do? They focus the worker on money, not high-quality work and the powerful motivation and satisfaction that comes from it. As J. Richard Hackman and Greg Oldham (1980) asserted, satisfaction is the result of good work, not the cause of it. Instead, the worker plots to beat the system to gain the next fix to buy the next toy. When pay and benefits are reasonable in comparison to other businesses and professions (market value), the satisfaction gained from doing good work well is lost, or the material rewards of work become the primary driver in one's life. People—in this case teachers—are baited with money to achieve greater productivity, and the focus on student welfare and producing learning becomes secondary. What we want are highly skilled teachers working cooperatively using proven methods with high-quality curricula to help students learn. When that happens the satisfaction and motivation to do even better results. Educators—all workers— then experience the wonderful spirit and rewards of good work (Frase & Conley, 1994). It is crucial to note, however, that when employees perceive pay and promotion procedures to be unfair the program will fail. We have observed outstanding teachers leaving the profession because they see the pay plan, both the single-salary schedule and ill-designed merit-pay plans, as unfair.

In 1992 (Frase), we used the story of Sisyphus from ancient mythology to illustrate the plight of teacher salary-schedule reformers. Sisyphus continually rolled big boulders up mountains; unfortunately, they all rolled back down. Salary-schedule reformers have the same foreboding challenge. They are rolling the same boulders, now sometimes called career ladders, differentiated staffing, incentive pay, or restructuring. To this point, the boulders have rolled back down the mountain. Here is what it will take to keep the boulders on top.

The Steps

The first step is to prepare teachers and school administrators adequately so that they are able to do their jobs well. We suggest starting by building

undergraduate teacher training and graduate administrative training programs on solid research evidence of what works and how to make good
decisions as contexts change. This is not now the case. While conducting
curriculum management audits across the nation and when talking with
our graduate administration students, we frequently heard from teachers
that the only instructional model they were taught in undergraduate
training was the Madeline Hunter model; although the model has inher-
ent value, it has earned *very little* support in the research literature. Administrators tell us that their training seldom reflected reality and frequently was a seemingly disjointed series of random philosophical
discussions. For administrators, a huge need is to learn the research literature on instruction, classroom management, and motivation and how to
analyze all of this in the classroom setting.

Second, teacher evaluators must be highly competent in instruction.
They must be able to analyze classroom settings, student–teacher interactions, and instructional activities. Personnel evaluation has top billing in
state statutes and school board policies, but as we said in chapter 8, the
real purpose—enhancing quality of work—is seldom realized. Principals
must be taught these skills, and their yearly training must focus on improving their abilities to foster instructional excellence. Further, they
must realize that the quality of teaching has a profound effect on student
achievement of all kinds, for example, standardized and criterion-referenced tests, portfolios, performances, and the like. Next, principals must
treat teachers as their next-in-line customer. Student achievement will be
little greater than the capacity of teachers to teach.

Third, we agree with Myron Lieberman (1993) and the Committee on
Economic Development (1994) that teacher pay should reflect prevailing,
regional labor markets, with higher pay for those with specialized skills.
When teachers with specialized skills are in short supply, they should receive higher pay so that the schools can compete in the marketplace. We
also suggest that when basing pay for individual teachers on their students' achievements cannot be accomplished, teachers should receive
group bonuses based on student achievement.

Fourth, principals should receive research data–driven training every
year on conducting sound analyses and assessments of instruction within
the context of the teacher's work environment. Training should also include developing sound suggestions for improvement (professional
growth plans), conducting conferences, and monitoring progress.

Fifth, each school board should require biannual reports from their superintendent for the purpose of determining the effectiveness of classroom instruction. If it is more effective, student achievement of some kind
should also be on the upswing. Continuous efforts must be made to improve education. The way to do this is to base educators' pay on the

amount of learning produced. The research conducted in Dallas linking teacher evaluation with student achievement speaks strongly in favor of its efficacy and validity (Mendro, 1998).

New ideas? Innovative? Hardly; it's all been tried before. In 1866, one year before Aaron Sheeley's call for performance-based pay, the parliament of Australia debated its practice of paying teachers an additional eight shillings for each child who passed the basic examination in literacy and numeracy and an extra four shillings for each child who passed in grammar and geography. It didn't last in Australia; today it suffers the same deadening impact of the single-salary schedule. The abundant attempts to introduce performance pay in America have gone down in flames. Witness Rochester's much-ballyhooed "restructuring" plan where many teachers received big pay raises. After three years of no improvement in student test scores or other evidence of increased learning, the school board and community shut it down. Witness the Fairfax merit pay plan. After much flamboyant wing-flapping, the union turned, the board changed, and the plan ended.

The unconscionable result of all of this is that the good and star teachers are the victims of the single-salary schedule. When confronted with a sterile and psychologically unsound compensation program, they eventually leave the classroom for something other than a teaching position—or they leave the profession entirely. The education systems, the students, and, ultimately, society are the losers.[8]

Notes

1. Cincinnati is one of the latest merit-pay programs to go down in flames. In this plan, all teachers in a school that attained its achievement targets were promised bonuses. See J. Archer (1999). "Cincinnati Teachers Rebuff Bonus-Pay Design." *Education Week,* vol. 17, no. 37, p. 5.

2. The authors recognize that teachers' pay also varies when extra pay schedule jobs are performed (e.g., coaching, student club sponsors, and so on).

3. For a thorough discussion of standardized testing and teaching to the test, see R. Stiggens (1999), "Assessment, Student Confidence, and School Success." *Phi Delta Kappan* 81(3), p. 191. Also see F. English (1999), *Deciding What to Teach and Test,* Newbury Park, CA: Corwin Press.

4. Study after study shows that many would-be teachers enter other fields simply because of the pay difference. These same studies show that many new teachers making $24,000 leave for higher paying jobs to provide homes for their families. In some school districts, such as the Compton Unified, auditors discovered that more than 50 percent of the teachers were on emergency credentials. The pay

was so low and the working conditions so bad that certified teachers could not be recruited (Frase, 1998).

5. For varied perspectives on the opinion, see Csikszentmihalyi (1997), Fox (1994), Herzberg (1966).

6. For a discussion of this topic see Bok (1993) and his rich series of references on this topic.

7. This topic has been discussed over the course of many centuries. The value of money as recognition may have a legitimate place in human resource management; however, it is misused as a motivator and its effects are overestimated. The following readings are recommended: Csikszentmihalyi (1990), Frase (1992), Hackman and Oldham (1980), and Herzberg (1966).

8. Some salary-schedule reformers are making improvements (Odden, 2000; Urbanski and Erskin, 2000). Unfortunately, they skirt the primary issue and perpetuate some of the underlying assumptions of this myth.

References

A Nation at Risk. (1983). Washington, DC: U.S. Department of Education. National Commission on Excellence in Education. David P. Gardner, Chairperson.

Bok, D. (1993). *The Cost of Talent*. New York: Free Press.

Bridge, R.G. (1979). *The Determinants of Educational Outcomes: The Impact of Families, Peers, Teachers, and Schools*. Cambridge: Ballinger.

Committee on Economic Development. (1994). *Putting Learning First*. New York: Committee on Economic Development.

Csikszentmihalyi, M. (1990). *Flow: The Psychology of Optimal Experience*. New York: Harper Perennial.

Csikszentmihalyi, M. (1997). *Finding Flow: The Psychology of Engagement with Everyday Life*. New York: Basic Books.

Davies, P. (1995). *About Time: Einstein's Unfinished Revolution*. New York: Simon and Schuster.

Epstein, Joyce. (1985). "A Question of Merit: Principals and Parents' Evaluations of Teachers." *Educational Researcher* (August/September 1985).

Fox, M. (1994). *Reinventing Work*. New York: Harper Collins.

Frase, L. (1992). *Teacher Motivation and Compensation*. Lancaster, PA: Technomic Publishing.

Frase, L., and S. Conley (1994). *Creating Learning Places for Teachers, Too*. Thousand Oaks, CA: Corwin Press.

Hackman, J., and G. Oldham (1980). *Work Redesign*. Menlo Park, CA: Addison-Wesley.

Havel, V. (1991). *Living in Truth*. Boston: Faber and Faber.

Herzberg, F. (1966). *Work and the Nature of Man*. Cleveland: World Publishing.

Lieberman, M. (1993). *Public Education: An Autopsy.* Cambridge: Harvard University Press.

Mendro, R. (1998). "Student Achievement and School Teacher Accountability." *Journal of Personnel Evaluation in Education* 12, pp. 257–267.

Mendro, R., H. Jordan, and K. Bembry. (1998). *An Application of Multiple Linear Regression in Determining Longitudinal Teacher Effectiveness.* Presented at the annual meeting of the American Education Research Association. San Diego, California.

Odden, A. (2000). "New and Better Forms of Teacher Compensation Are Possible." *Phi Delta Kappan* 81(5), p. 361.

Peck, S. (1995). *Gifts for the Journey.* San Francisco: Harper San Francisco.

Sheldrake, R. (1994). *The Rebirth of Nature.* Rochester, VT: Park Street Press.

Stigler, R. (1997). *The TIMSS Videotape Classroom Study: Methods and Preliminary Findings.* ZEUS School District: Office of Educational Research and Improvement, U.S. Department of Education.

Urbanski, A., and R. Erskin. "School Reform, TURN, and Teacher Compensation." *Phi Delta Kappan* 81(5), p. 367.

Wilms, W., and R. Chapleau. (1999). "The Illusion of Paying Teachers for Student Performance." *Education Week* 19, no. 10, p. 48.

MYTH 10:
LARGE SCHOOLS PROVIDE QUALITY EDUCATION EFFICIENTLY FOR LARGE NUMBERS OF STUDENTS

Introduction

In 1994, the *New York Times* announced again that graduates of small rural schools in the Midwest and West are the top performers in the nation when it comes to the SAT and ACT, the widely reported college entrance examinations (Johnson, 1994). The astonishing part of this is that educators tend to disregard this phenomenon. They attribute it to racial homogeneity or to strong traditional values in these small heartland farming towns. These attitudes, whether they are founded in nostalgia or latent racism, ignore a large body of research developed over the past half-century that says children—all children—do better in small schools. According to a study by the American Legislative Exchange Council (Feistrizer, 1993), the rural schools are doing better because they are *small*, not because they are a particular culture or race. The study goes on to explain that when the data are disaggregated and analyzed by race, minority children in small rural schools outperform their counterparts in the rest of the nation. The study concluded that small school size was even more important than small classroom size in the performance of students.

Is it possible that a country intent on improving education could overlook overwhelming evidence pointing the way to vastly improved schools? America's top performers are states well known for their abundance of small towns and small schools—Iowa, Kansas, Minnesota, Montana, Nebraska, North Dakota, South Dakota, Utah, Wisconsin, Wyoming—all regularly in the top ten of performing states in the nation.

The Myth

Shortly after America was stunned by Sputnik in 1957, American educators were confronted with a plethora of suggestions about how to reform education in order to catch up with the Soviets. Foremost among these was a widely circulated report by James Conant, a highly regarded Harvard professor, containing twenty-one ways American high schools could change to meet the challenge.[1] Conant speculated that a major problem in the country at that time was the existence of high schools too small to allow a diversified curriculum except at "exorbitant expense." He declared, "The prevalence of such high schools—those with graduating classes of less than 100 students—constitutes one of the serious obstacles to good secondary education throughout most of the United States." He worried that these schools did not fulfill the American dream of a comprehensive high school serving both the vocationally oriented and the academically talented. A small high school, he argued, cannot by its very nature offer a comprehensive curriculum, and it uses uneconomically the time and efforts of administrators, teachers, and specialists. Conant felt that a high school must have at least 750 students so that classes in advanced subjects and separate advanced classes within all subjects could be possible. He urged consolidation of small school districts and small schools.

Schools all over the nation jumped on the bandwagon, anxious to do their part in fending off the Evil Empire. Educators embraced the idea that large schools at all levels could provide more specialized services for children more cost-effectively. School leaders immediately pointed out the major advantages to large schools. First, the larger student populations meant that there would always be sufficient students to support ability grouping of students at the various grade levels. For example, the first grade could be divided into a "high first" and a "low first," reducing the differences in the total range of achievement with which a teacher would cope. Moreover, class sizes in larger schools would tend to be better balanced with less combination classes, and students who were retained could spend the second year in another teacher's class. Put another way, the entrenched practices of grouping, grading, and sorting students were solidly supported by the large-school push. At both the elementary and the secondary levels, special courses could be offered. Elementary libraries could be economically staffed, and the necessity for itinerant art, music, speech-therapy, and reading teachers would be eliminated. Large high schools could have magnificent marching bands and orchestras, well-developed choirs and drama programs, and powerful athletic teams. Administrative staffs could expand to include specialists of various sorts. At the same time, the leadership teams would be more stable, supposedly because good administrators would not be constantly searching for positions in larger schools with more status and salary. Board members were easily convinced that larger schools were more cost-effective.

The majority of the research on school size and cost during the years following Conant's report focused on senior high schools and echoed Conant's concern that a graduating class must have at least one hundred students in order to provide proper breadth in the curriculum. Conant's prestige, coupled with Admiral Hyman Rickover's dire warnings of impending doom at the hands of the Soviets, left an indelible print on American education. Other studies focused on district size, primarily related to cost, and even though researchers were unable to turn up convincing evidence of the cost-effectiveness of large districts, the stampede was on. Ten years after the alarm had been sounded, school systems across the nation had made major moves to consolidate. California, which had 3,400 school districts earlier in the century, reduced the number to less than 1,500. In 1997, that number had been reduced still further to 1,023, in spite of the fact that the state more than doubled its student population. Later, while politicians and school leaders were frantically reorganizing their districts and curriculum, no one seemed to notice that graduates from the old school systems placed men on the moon and propelled our nation into the space age far ahead of the pesky Russians. But Conant's common-sensical speculations about the size of school organizations stuck. Americans were convinced that big schools were better.

In the 1960s and 1970s, it was widely believed that large school districts and large schools promoted racial integration and equitable funding. School districts would be able to draw racially balanced attendance boundaries, and school districts that encompassed both sides of the railroad tracks would create more equitable school funding. The issue of very wealthy districts living next door to very poor districts inspired the *Serrano v. Priest* decision (issued by the California Supreme Court; see Elmore and McLaughlin, 1981) concerning the question of equity in school funding. The idea that the quality of a student's education should not be determined by the neighborhood in which he or she lives rapidly spread to more than half the states in America and, with it, the notion that building larger school organizations would help solve the problems of social disparity.

The Reality

Research on school size consistently supports the notion that students in small schools perform better academically than those in large schools (Fowler and Walberg, 1991). A study on the reading performance of K–12 students in the United States not only reported that students in small schools read better, but students in schools with populations of two hundred or fewer engage in *twice* as much reading practice as those in schools with populations of one thousand or more (Paul, 1996). Reading is a learned skill—arguably the most important academic skill learned in school. Like any skill, the more you practice, the better you become. The better academic performance of students in small schools can be traced to a better opportunity to practice and learn the most basic of our basic skills.

It is often difficult to point out with certainty those factors that cause students to succeed in school and later life. For example, in Chapter 6 we discuss the research on forcing children to repeat grades. On the surface the idea sounded good. After all, what could be wrong with setting clear expectations with clear consequences for failure? But careful study over many years has revealed that retaining slow learners does more harm than good. And much of the harm done to the children involves their socialization, the way they see themselves in their school world, and the roles they think they must play. We simply can't ignore the fact that a large part of a child's acculturation results from interaction with the school society—the other children. These are dynamics at work in schools that professional educators must heed. Children's attitudes and interests are influenced by their interactions with a peer society at school shaped by a multitude of factors, not the least of which is the number of students attending the school.

There is a consistent body of evidence, gathered over the last half-century and largely ignored, that indicates the dynamics at work in big schools restrict the individual growth of their students. Conant's report failed to consider that it takes much more than an accumulation of a large number of people in one place to achieve a program that truly provides for individual differences. In fact, just the opposite occurs. Research in other social settings has established that students in large schools actually have less direct contacts with classmates than students in smaller school settings, while research on cognitive complexity revealed that small-school students enter a wider range of behavior settings and have more responsible positions in these settings than do students of large schools.[2]

A San Francisco area superintendent recently opened his own high school yearbook and counted the number of students participating in athletics, music programs, drama, student government, and other so-called extracurricular activities that add rich meaning to a student's school experience. It was not surprising to him to find that 370 students had been involved in extracurricular activity to some significant degree during the school year. This represented more than 80 percent of the 450-student high school's population. Why such high participation? Because there is a place in the small school for all students. In those days, the superintendent recalled, nearly every able-bodied boy with any size was on the varsity, junior varsity, or freshman football teams in the fall. Girls at that time were also heavily involved in volleyball or the drill team. Other boys and girls ran cross-country or prepared for winter or spring sports. Most of these same students participated in drama and doubled as musicians in the band or choir, in addition to duties as class officers and club members. Otherwise, there wouldn't be enough students to conduct these important programs. Coaches and band directors did not demand that their students choose between athletics and music, as they did in the superintendent's large urban high schools. Rather, they accommodated both interests. Students felt needed and important. Their budding talents were needed and appreciated.

New students enrolling in these small-school settings were immediately caught up in the school's culture. Since the overwhelming majority of the student body was involved with school activities, the classes consequently were composed primarily of *involved* students. New students experienced nearly "total immersion" in a culture characterized by involvement in healthy, school-related enterprises. Moreover, from the beginning students were encouraged to participate in more than one activity. School, for these small–high school students, was more likely to be the central focus of their adolescent lives.

When the superintendent contrasted this educational setting with his modern comprehensive high schools, he was dismayed by what he saw. In one of his large (1,500-student) high schools, more than 600 students were involved in a large variety of school settings. The big difference, of course, was the huge number of noninvolved students.

An earlier landmark study of the impact of school size supported the superintendent's observations (Barker and Gump, 1964). The study found that large-school students were exposed on average to 189 educational settings but achieved only in 3.5. In the small school, the student was exposed to only 48 settings but achieved in 8.6—*nearly 2.5 times more.*

Another study found that as high schools approach seven hundred pupils, they appear to provide most of the activities of larger schools but offer students many more opportunities to participate.[3] A decline of opportunity for participation begins somewhere around eight hundred and continues until the school reaches a low point at the 1,500-student level, after which "only a slight drop in the magnitude of student involvement was distinguishable." By the time the student body reaches 1,500, the large high school phenomenon of semidetachment has been firmly established for a large number of the students.

As a school grows, the number of noninvolved "outsiders" grows exponentially. Roger Barker and Paul Gump (1964) found that in large schools there nearly always was a sizable group of outsiders. No such group was found in the small schools they studied. They also found, when they compared the largest school in their study to the smallest, that the larger school had sixty-five times as many students but only eight times as many settings. Moreover, there were only 1.5 times as many varieties of settings in the largest school. In other words, big schools could offer specialized courses such as string ensembles, and although this was not feasible for the small schools, at least one course of this *variety* was offered—usually band or orchestra. This suggests that while we thought in the past that a large school provides a more varied program, the evidence would indicate that the variation is slight.

The Outsiders

What difference does this all make? Simply this: in the large school it is the marginal students who tend to become the noninvolved outsiders— the misfits, the gang members. Academically marginal students in large schools have a very different experience than those in small schools. In the small school their marginal characteristics make no difference in their participation in activities. These students are able to experience almost as many activities as other students. The dynamics of the society in which they find themselves push them toward participation. In the large school, marginal students experience less pressure toward participation and are much more likely to become outsiders. One study reported by Barker and Gump found that the proportionate number of student leaders decreases also as school size increases (Kleinert, 1969). The result is a double whammy. Big schools push the marginal student out while they discourage the development of leadership among those who remain.

The bulk of the research shows that small schools do at least as well as large schools in terms of standardized test scores, and some reports, such as the report of the SAT scores mentioned above, would suggest small schools actually perform consistently better. None of this is a surprise to modern social scientists. Since World War II, research on depth and range of human participation clearly outlined the characteristic behavior of people in smaller organizations[4]:

- They are absent less often.
- They quit their jobs less often.
- They are more punctual.
- When asked to volunteer, they participate more frequently.
- They function in positions of responsibility and importance more frequently and in a wider range of activities.
- When compared with members of larger group organizations, they are more productive.
- They demonstrate more leadership behavior.

When asked about their experiences, people in small organizations reported the following about their organizations:

- They receive more satisfaction.
- They find their work more meaningful.
- They are more satisfied with payment schemes.
- They more often feel that participation in the organization had been valuable and useful.

The Cost of Operating Small Schools

Common sense, or so it seems, would tell us that larger schools are more cost-effective on a per-pupil basis. Actually, except for very small schools (under one hundred students), per-pupil costs don't vary much. However, as the enrollment climbs, there is more need for combating the negative impact of the increased student population. Larger schools need more special education programs for the educationally handicapped and students who cannot, for one reason or another, adapt to the larger school setting. Increased discipline problems require additional administrators, counselors, and psychologists.

In 1998, researchers from New York University found that alternative high schools with fewer than six hundred students were actually more cost-effective in terms of producing graduates than larger, traditional schools. Most previous studies of educational costs found large schools to be less expensive on a per-pupil basis. But when educational outcomes were considered—when schools were compared on a *per-graduate* basis—the smaller schools cost less.[5]

Even adding additional facilities to the district's inventory does not create a major financial barrier. The cost per square foot of building a school for three hundred students is not appreciably different from that of building a one thousand–student school. It is true that at the high school level special facilities like band rooms, gymnasiums, and stadiums will be duplicated for each of the small schools, because more students will be participating in more settings. But think about that for a moment. Isn't that what educators are trying to accomplish? Large schools have a tendency to concentrate upon extracurricular goals and standards that can be achieved only by the more talented students. Small schools cast a wider net. As a result, large schools have a more difficult time achieving a sense of attachment and contribution to group goals among the students. "No school spirit" is a common complaint among large-school student leaders. No doubt distributing students among smaller schools would increase participation in a variety of settings and require expanded facilities—arguably well worth the extra expense.

Much has been written about what happens to the noninvolved outsiders. Included in this hapless group of students are the dropouts (even though many of them attend for four years) and the gang members. Certainly we cannot blame all of America's social ills on the size of its schools, but some of the additional costs to society accrued by dropouts must be added to the costs of operating large school facilities. We believe small schools would help stem the tide of alienated, antisocial citizens and reduce the enormous monetary and social costs associated with crime and poverty in our country.

The Impact of Large Schools on Teachers

And what about the teachers? Large organizations restrict the individual with regard to what Chris Argyris once called "the attainment of vestiges of adulthood" (Argyris, 1996). In other words, it is difficult for the individual in a subordinate status in a large chain of command to develop a feeling of self-worth relative to the institution. Large school districts are not exempt from this unsavory aspect of bureaucracy. The tendency of a large school organization to drive the individual toward a dependent position is another impact of large school size. Large school district organizations have a tendency to be more "closed" organizations and generally less responsive to the stakeholders. Administrators within these organizations are more evasive, more worrying, more lacking in tolerance, more submissive, more dependent, more conventional, and more easily upset than principals in smaller organizations with "open" climates.[6]

Research findings related to the adverse effect of large school size on school climate have been among our profession's best-kept secrets. We conducted a study of organizational climate as reported by more than six hundred California school administrators from large and small districts. Our analyses revealed dramatically that large district organizational climates tend to be "closed," while small districts tend to be more "open." Even more distressing news was that big district central offices exhibited generally closed organizational climates and fostered these closed climates in the bulk of their schools. This means, according to the research on open and closed organizational climates, that large school districts are less flexible, less productive, less innovative, and less responsive to the needs of the community.

No one was surprised three decades ago when the Great Plains Study concluded that "it becomes increasingly difficult and sometimes seemingly impossible to communicate information adequately and to coordinate social activities effectively as political units grow to exceed an optimum size" (Levine and Havigurst, 1968). For nearly a half-century we have known that the processes of leadership are adversely affected by increased organizational size. For example, in industry we learned that as organizations grow larger communication patterns involve less of the membership. Conversely, the leadership element assumes a larger share of the communication activities. In other words, as the organization expands, the communication patterns tend gradually to centralize around fewer and fewer central leaders, through whom most of the information flows. This problem in the context of large school districts was formally recognized by the American Association of School Administrators as early as 1944. The association's yearbook prominently noted that most large school districts had become autocratic in the interest of efficiency, even though the professed policy was democratic. Fifty years later, large districts are still struggling in vain to implement democratic management models called "participatory management," or "site-based management," or "total quality management," or whatever the latest binge is labeled. Almost without exception they fail.

The Solution

It is no surprise that Iowa's small rural schools are leading the league in college-entrance exam scores or that their dropout rate is low. Smaller school size is clearly an advantage to students. Organizational experts are clear that smaller units operate more effectively and are more capable of coping successfully with a variety of changing requirements in a fast-moving society than are the large organizations. Nowhere is this more important than in the intensive human relations business we call education. Personnel problems of small staffs are less frequent and lesser in magnitude. The incidents of hard-core negotiations and the devastation of labor union turmoil, rigid contract agreements, complex grievance procedures, and expensive legal proceedings are reduced. Small schools tend to have a higher ratio of citizen–patron support of the school's operation, and smaller faculties can be expected to foster healthier community relationships and closer ties with the citizenry.

With all these advantages, it would seem that teachers and administrators would join in a dynamic chorus demanding the benefits of smaller school size. Quite the contrary. Educators are their own worst enemies. Principals and superintendents climbing the administrative hierarchy are seeking the status of larger schools and larger districts. Coaches and booster clubs enjoy the status of the big-school competition and recognize the advantage of a larger pool of talent in a big school. Band directors, choir directors, and drama coaches also feed on the large talent pool available in the big school. Classroom teachers thrive on the specialized gifted and honors sections in their subjects, and on and on. In other words, in spite of the many recognized virtues of the smaller school organization, the greatest resistance to breaking up the big schools would come from within and would quickly garner the support of the elite in the community—the parents of the gifted performers and athletes. Few would stand to defend the interests of the noninvolved outsiders. In the community, discussion of smaller schools meets with skepticism. The commonsensical notion that "big" means "more efficient" prevails. Somehow, the practice of packing the students into heavy concentrations (see the cartoon) makes sense to the person on the street. Moreover, many of our successful, active citizens have the attitude, "We made it, and we attended large schools." Of course, those who didn't make it aren't saying anything, and those who could have done better probably don't realize it.

Public schools are a function of the legislature of each state. These governmental bodies have the responsibility of creating and dissolving local districts and establishing rules and guidelines to ensure that high-quality education is delivered to the children of their states. The question of how large we should allow our districts, schools, and classes to become before we establish new districts, schools, or classes can be easily and directly addressed by the legislatures. Many states control class sizes already. Of course, local districts can also address the problem of school size—and many have. Local districts, however, often lack the political stability or personal conviction to maintain school size policies over the course of many years, and policies affecting growth and facilities planning require political staying power. At the local level, school finances too often are a real or imagined barrier. Besides, state legislators are increasingly under the gun of the state courts to ensure an even level of educational quality throughout their states. Leaving a quality question of this magnitude to the whimsy of local school boards would not be fully responsible (see Chapter 4).

Politicians tend to be blinded by the seemingly logical argument that big schools cost less, and they are unable to factor in the cost of the human wreckage in our jails, our inner-city gangs, and the welfare roles. Sooner or later we must comprehend that the customary popular notions about how big our schools should be are not adequate bases for policy decisions. We need to act on what we know. Schools must be sufficiently small that *all* of the students feel needed.

Notes

1. Conant's report proposed a classic intensification and expansion of the curriculum of the comprehensive high school. Entitled *The American High School Today* (New York: McGraw-Hill, 1959), it played a major role in the public school response to the Soviet Sputnik threat in 1957 to America's technological superiority. We have noted that most politically motivated reform movements over the last four decades have been centered around intensification of existing models of schooling rather than redevelopment of programs based on advanced research.

2. For a discussion of student alternatives in a large high school, read Alan Glathorn's article entitled, "Individual Self-fulfillment in the Large High School" (*NASSP Bulletin* 335, March 1969). Also insightful is Allan Wicker's "Cognitive Complexity, School Size, and Participation in School Settings" (*Journal of Educational Psychology*, June 1969).

3. In 1982, the ERIC Clearinghouse on Educational Management published a review of the impact of school size on students entitled, *A Reassessment of the Small School* (Eugene, OR: The Clearinghouse). Another study by John Kleinert focused on student participation at various levels of student population. This study, entitled "Effects of High School Size on Student Activity Participation," was reported in the March 1969 *NASSP Bulletin*.

4. In their compendium of studies on school size (*Big School, Small School*, 1964), Barker and Gump cited organizational studies during the previous thirty-year pe-

riod that were relevant to the research on school organizations. They concluded that in relatively underpopulated settings individuals expend more effort in a wider range of activities than in heavily populated settings. Moreover, individuals in underpopulated settings have a higher frequency of difficult and important functions. Barker and Gump postulated that these organizational characteristics were relevant in the school setting and affected quality of education.

5. The *New York Times* carried a report of the New York University study on the cost of small alternative schools on May 5, 1998, p. A26.

6. In 1972, we conducted organizational climate research aimed at large and small school districts. The classic *Organizational Climate Description Questionnaire* (originally developed by Halpin and Croft) was modified for upper echelon school district administrators

References

Argyris, C. (1996). *Organizational Learning II: Theory, Method, and Practice.* Reading, MA: Addison-Wesley Publishing Company.

Barker, R., and P. Gump (1964). *Big School, Small School.* Stanford, CA: Stanford University Press.

Elmore, R., and M. McLaughlin (1981). *Reform and Retrenchment: The Politics of California School Finance Reform.* Santa Monica, CA: Rand Corporation.

Feistrizer, C. (1993). *Report Card on American Education.* Washington, DC: American Legislative Exchange Council.

Fowler, W., and H. Walberg (1991). "School Size, Characteristics, and Outcomes." *Educational Evaluation and Policy Analysis* 13(2).

Johnson, D. "Study Says Small Schools Are Key to Learning." *New York Times*, September 21, 1994, p. B12.

Kleinert, J. (1969). "Effects of High School Size on Student Activity Participations." *NASSP Bulletin*, 53(335): 34.

Levine, D., and R. Havigurst (1968). *Emerging Urban Problems and Their Significance for School District Organization in the Great Plains States.* Columbia: University of Missouri Press.

Paul, T. (1996). *Patterns of Reading Practice.* Madison, WI: The Institute for Academic Excellence.

Index

accountability, xi
    cost of reforms, xv
    A Nation at Risk, 16
    National Education Standards, 16
    Ronald Reagan and, 16
administrators
    training, 96, 99, 112
authentic assessment, 21

behaviorism, 16
    Admiral Hyman Rickover and, 17
Bergson, Henri, 111
Boards of Education, vii, xi, 1, 10, 11, 13
    history, 41, 43–46
    ineptitude, 46–52
    legislatures and, 46
    macromanagement and, 52
    merit pay, 112
    origin, 39
    quality of, 54
    roles, 41, 44, 47–48, 52, 99
    teacher evaluation, 99–100
    as a vestigial remain, 40
Boston Latin School, 84

California curriculum framework, 21
character education, 85
Child Development Project, 86
collective bargaining, 30
Chuang Tzu Tao, 111
curriculum management audit, 49, 50,
    55, 99–100, 107

diversification, excessive, 6–10
dropouts, 60, 71

education
    economics, vii–x
    problems, xi
    purpose of, 1–10, 43, 44, 47–48, 52, 57
        merit pay and, 112
        teacher evaluation and, 99, 112

First Amendment, 81

Galileo, ix
grades and grading, 66
    bell curve, 75
    Chicago School Board and, 59, 69
    cheating, 71
    college prep classes, 73
    dropouts, 60, 71
    valedictorians, 70
    weights and grades, 70
grouping, 65–77
    Pop Warner syndrome, 73

William and Henry Hewlett Founda-
    tion, 86

Job skills
    African-American parents and, 61
    Asian parents and, 61
    Latino parents and, 60
    White parents and, 61

Lake Woebegone effect, 96
legislator
    myths and, 7
    teacher tenure, due process, and, 99

macromanagement, 52
merit pay, 103–115
    history, 106, 108, 111, 113
    objectivity, 109
    regional labor markets and, 112
    student achievement and, 109–110
    sisyphus and, 111
micromanagement, 52
motivation, 110–111
    external
        teacher unions and, 27–37
        variations due to income, 110
    internal
        St. Thomas Aquinas and, 111
        teachers and, 111
        work and, 111
Myths
    criteria for selecting top ten, xiii–xv
    definition of, xi–xiii, xv
    regarding IQ tests, xii–xiii
    newspapers and, xi, 6
    the Sandia Laboratories report, ix–x
    purposes of, vii–xiii
        Plato, xii
        Santa Claus, xii

National Defense Education Act, 17
    Franklin Delano Roosevelt and, 28
National Education Standards, 16
National Public Relations Board, 33

parenting
    role in education xii, xi, 10, 11, 60
    Indochinese student success, 62
    responsibility, 63
Plato, xii
principals
    duties, 99
    evaluation of teachers, 94–95
program management audits, 23

retention, 68, 73

Sandi National Laboratories, ix
Size, school
    academic performance and, 120
    consolidation of districts, 119

cost-effectiveness and, 119, 123–124
course of study and, 121
extracurricular activities and, 121
noninvolved students and outsiders,
    122
school climate
    teachers in large schools, 125
self-esteem, 57
    academics and, 60–61
    African American students, 60–61
    Asian students, 61
    education and, 58–59
    hard work and, 62
    Latino parents and, 60
    as a result of learning, 59, 62
Shanker, Albert, xi, 29
single-salary schedule, 103, 104, 108
society, 9
special education, 66, 80
    attention deficit disorder, 72
    behavior disorder, 67
    gifted, 67
    honors, 67
    learning disabled, 67
    resource specialist, 67
Sputnik, 17
    Friends of Education, 118
stick to your knitting philosophy
    In education, 7–10
    Anthony and Cleopatra, 7
superintendents, x, 10, 11
    policy role in teacher evaluation, 99
    setting administrative priorities, 99

teacher evaluation, 93–115
    accuracy, 94–96
    efficacy of, 106–108
    laws and legal compliance, 94, 97
    politics of, 97–98
    purpose, 93–94
    school principals' conduct, 96
    training teacher evaluators, 98
teacher training
    merit pay, 111–112
    student achievement, 59, 100
teachers
    competency, 95

dismissal, 95, 99
duties, 45–46
tenure, 95
testing
  high stakes, 16
  IQ tests, xii–xiii, 19
    Alfred Binet, xii
  Japanese style testing, 76
  misuse of in relationship to learning,
    v–vi
  standardized, 17
    Abraham Maslow, 20
    merit pay, 106
  statewide testing programs
Third International Maths and Science
  Study, 19, 107
Thomas Aquinas, Saint, 111
truancy, 11
two-class school system, xii
  Alfred Binet and, xii

unions
  adversarial relations, 36
  AFL/CIO, 28
  American Federation of Teachers, 29
    John F. Kennedy, 30
  collaboration with management, 30
  collective bargaining, 30

George Meany, 28
industrial style negotiations, 33
National Education Association, 36,
  57
Ken Parker, 29
paternalism, 29
Public employee unions, 28
new unionism, 36
Albert Shanker, 29
teacher, 28

Values
  American, 82
  Boston Latin School, 84
  City Montessori School, 87
  Judeo-Christian morality, 81
    Mahatma Gandhi, 87
  prosocial literature, 87
  public agenda, 84
  separation of church and state, 81
    Oliver Wendell Holmes and, 84
  traditional values, 82
  Ten Commandments, 80
    William Inge and, 80
  values education, 83
  Waldorf education, 88

wants of students, 59–60
workplace basics, 18

About the Authors

Larry E. Frase is the author or editor of 80 professional journal articles and 22 books, including *School Management by Wandering Around* (1990); *Maximizing People Power in Schools* (1992); *Teacher Compensation and Motivation* (1992); and *Creating Learning Places for Teachers, Too* (1994). He has served as a teacher; as assistant superintendent for elementary schools in the Uniondale Union Free School District on Long Island for two years; as assistant superintendent for educational services (K–12) in the Flowing Wells School District in the Tucson, Arizona, area; and as superintendent of the Catalina Foothills School District in the Tucson, Arizona, area.

Frase is a vice president and a senior lead auditor for the Curriculum Management Audit Center. He has served as lead auditor on 30 curriculum management audits in small, large, and inner-city school districts. Frase has served as auditor on 15 curriculum management audits.

Frase is professor of educational administration, College of Education, San Diego State University. He serves as consultant to school districts in areas such as teacher and administrator motivation, alternative pay plans, and work environment assessment and enhancement. He serves as keynote speaker for professional associations in Canada and the United States.

William A. Streshly is professor and chair for the Department of Administration, Rehabilitation, and Postsecondary Education at San Diego State University. Before coming to the university, Professor Streshly spent 30 years in public school administration, including 5 years as principal of a large suburban high school and 14 years as superintendent of three California school districts varying in size from 2,500 to 25,000 students.

Professor Streshly has published articles on character education, staff development, curriculum management, competency testing, school finance, and school labor relations. He is also coauthor of a practical book on school law titled *Avoiding Legal Hassles* and a book on teacher unions

133

titled *Teacher Unions and Total Quality Education.* He has served as speaker or consultant for more than thirty state and national conferences, school districts, and professional organizations, in addition to scores of speaking engagements for community service clubs, Chambers of Commerce, alumni clubs, and political groups. He has been active in the leadership of numerous community/civic organizations and has served as an educational adviser to county, state, and federal officials.